TRAPS
OF TREASURE

THE ESSENTIAL PRIMER TO NAVIGATE THE INVESTMENT WORLD'S RIGGED PLAYING FIELD

Louis Scherschel

ISBN 978-1-63814-599-8 (Paperback)
ISBN 978-1-63814-600-1 (Hardcover)
ISBN 978-1-63814-601-8 (Digital)

Copyright © 2021 Louis Scherschel
All rights reserved
First Edition

All rights reserved. No part of this publication may be reproduced, distributed, or transmitted in any form or by any means, including photocopying, recording, or other electronic or mechanical methods without the prior written permission of the publisher. For permission requests, solicit the publisher via the address below.

Covenant Books
11661 Hwy 707
Murrells Inlet, SC 29576
www.covenantbooks.com

Disclaimer

The contents of and statements made in *Traps of Treasure* solely reflect the opinions and experiences of Louis Scherschel alone. The material in *Traps of Treasure* is neither a recommendation nor an endorsement of any investment product, strategy, or entity and is not to be interpreted as offering investment advice. Nor is it to be construed as any form of advertisement or solicitation for business. Louis Scherschel does not provide tax, investment, or legal advice. All decisions regarding the tax or legal implications of your investments should be made in connection with your independent tax, investment, or legal advisor.

All views expressed are the opinions of Louis Scherschel based solely on his past experience in the wealth management field. No guarantee of any outcome is ever implied. All opinions contained in *Traps of Treasure* constitute Louis Scherschel's beliefs as of the date of publication, are subject to change without notice, and are provided in good faith but without legal responsibility.

Past performance is not a guide to future performance, future returns are not guaranteed, and a loss of original capital when investing may occur. Louis Scherschel does not accept any liability whatsoever for any direct or consequential loss arising from any information contained herein. No material contained in this document may be reproduced or copied by any means without the prior consent of Louis Scherschel. Copyright © Louis Scherschel 2022. All rights reserved.

For my grandfather, Louis Kamaski, the man who instilled in me the enduring value of moral living, Main Street values, loyalty, and hard work. May his hard-earned labors and memory live on through my efforts.

CONTENTS

Introduction
Seeing Is Believing..11
- Educating the General Retail Investor 12
- Wealth Management Industry Framework 12
- Your Financial Professional.......................................13
- Internal Advisor Changes 13
- Moral Investment Management, Not Just Ethical 14
- Philosophical Strategies and Product Types 15
- Fraud and Proper Communication 16
- Fake News..17
- Keeping Up with Your Peers......................................18
- Reinventing the Wheel...19

Chapter 1
The Road to Damascus
Figuring Out Your Path..21
- Independent Broker, Wire House, RIA, or DIY 22
  - The independent broker 22
  - The wire house 24
  - RIA (registered investment advisor) 27
  - DIY (do-it-yourself) 29
- Money Manager or Middleman—Which Kind of Advisor Do You Have? 33
  - Defining the money manager 34
  - The middleman passing game..................................35
  - Costs of a money manager or middleman 36

- The Puppet or the Ventriloquist: Client Facing or Back Office—Know Who Is Speaking to You 37
  - The back office 37
  - Product peddling 39

Chapter 2
Winds of Change
When Change Can Help or Harm 41
- Musical Brokers 42
  - Payout structures 43
  - Overbearing compliance 44
  - Client poachers 45
- Revolving Advisors 46
  - Making the cut 46
  - Advisor-firm stipulated agreements 47
- Advisor Longevity: Prudent Lengths of Time when Selecting an Advisor 49
  - Affiliation rotation 49
- Broker Protocol: Friend to the Firm, Foe to the Advisor and Investor 51
  - Clean breaks? Not always. 51
  - Who controls the relationship? Firm, advisor, or client? 52

Chapter 3
Moral Obligation to Moral Hazard
Conflicts in the Wealth Accumulation Process 54
- Discretionary 55
  - Trading approvals 55
  - Excessive risk 56
- Nondiscretionary 57
  - Client makes the call. 57
  - Additional directives 58
- Fiduciary 59
  - Serving the faithful 59
  - Finding a fiduciary advisor. 60

- Nonfiduciary 61
  - The lesser standard 61
  - Suitability versus fiduciary 62
  - Regulatory roulette 62

Chapter 4
Who Is in the Details—God or the Devil?
Techniques for Consideration...64
- Active versus Passive Management: The Endless Battle...65
  - Which one to choose 66
  - Passive management 66
  - Active management 67
  - The mechanical details 68
  - Strategy interference and surprises 69
- Technocrat or Psychologist: Harnessing both for Prudent Investing...70
  - The technocrat 71
  - The psychologist 72
- The Investment Product Buffet..73
  - The specialist or generalist advisor 73
  - Accredited investing..74

Chapter 5
Camels through Needle Eyes
Industry Problems of Self-Interest and Fraud.......................76
- Who's Watching the Watchers?..78
  - Policy deception 78
  - Regulatory teeter-totter..79
- Broker Fraud or Attorney Fraud—Discern the Difference 80
  - Statement verification and churning 80
  - Legal extortion..81
  - Background checks 82
  - An exploitative business model 84
- Caller, You're <u>Not</u> on the Line!......................................85
  - The advisor's muzzle 85
  - Big brother compliance..86

Chapter 6
I Will Not Set Before My Eyes Anything That Is Worthless
Media Manipulations 88
- The Headline Du Jour: Media Mania 89
  - Internal information 90
  - Unreliable data 90
  - Recycled headlines 92
  - Sourcing your own data 92
- Stop Chasing the Hot Dot! 94
  - Building and culling the herd 94
  - Nascent performance memory 95
  - Roller-coaster parabolas 96

Chapter 7
Theories of Relativity
Misunderstandings and Misrepresentations 99
- Investing Is Easy—That's Why Everyone Is a Multimillionaire..100
  - Professional reprogramming 101
  - The physician's syndrome 102
- I Have This Friend Who— 103
  - The unproven returns...104
- The Enclaves versus the Other 95 Percent...................105
  - Break down your time frames 106
  - Comparison conundrum 106

Chapter 8
Moving Goalposts
The Industry's Continuous Reinvention....................................108
- The Never-Ending Growth Chart................................109
  - Short-term investment evaporation........................110
  - Your investing life span..110
- Dangling Carrots 111
  - Self-trading with robo-advisors 111
  - Get a third-party perspective..................................112

- Theoretical Rotation: MPT and Sixty-Forty................113
  - Alternative theoretical strategies............................114

Chapter 9
Incorruptible
Summary Points for Diving into Wealth Management................116
- A Good Starting Point 117
- Minimum Expectations of Privacy and Account Security..119
  - Client privacy 120
  - Information we collect...121
  - Third parties to whom we disclose information 122
  - Our firm's Business Continuity Plan.......................123
  - Differences between investment brokerage firms and banks 123
  - Sufficient measures to protect your assets................124

Conclusion...127

Appendix A
List of General Retail Investment Accounts and Products............129

Appendix B
Critical Questions to Ask a Financial Advisor or Investment Firm..132

INTRODUCTION

Seeing Is Believing

Faith and trust. These are two basic principles of any belief system, whether they involve religious, marital, professional, personal, or coaching relationships. It is said that faith is belief in the absence of proof or the ability to see for oneself. One area where faith and trust become critical to everyday life lies in the realm of finance and personal investments.

In today's world, many entrust their hard-earned money and life savings to a broad array of professionals within the financial services field. These professionals take many forms, from private wealth managers to insurance agents to tax professionals and so forth. Yet how is the average retail investor supposed to know who to trust and believe? As a matter of standard practice, the public is bombarded daily with infomercials, commercials, and downright fraudulent advertisement. Self-serving financial advisors or banking practitioners often only seek to serve themselves by bombarding the general public with information overload.

Traps of Treasure discusses numerous practices within the investment advisory sector that are not often seen or revealed to the general public. Much of what goes on within the investment management field is intentionally obscured through smoke and mirrors. The individual investor is left feeling like the characters of the *Wizard of Oz*, wondering who the all-powerful Oz is and what the source of influence is. Much to their dismay, they discover that Oz is nothing more than a charlatan pulling levers behind a curtain so his methods are not discovered.

Educating the General Retail Investor

The intent of this book is neither to advocate for nor against particular financial products and technical strategies. An excess of prognosticators and talking heads can easily be found on television paid programming or financial websites. Each vies for attention and the general public's monetary contributions. Those prognosticators also frequently end up contradicting one another in the hopes that they can gain the upper hand in securing your subscription of easy payments to enrich their own extravagant lifestyles.

Rather, the contents herein attempt to provide the novice investor, and those seeking deeper insight, valuable perspective into what often happens in large investment firms. Legal actions, marketing, and internal relationships of financial professionals are just a few areas not clearly viewed by the general public's eye. With additional insight, you will hopefully be provided necessary tools to begin your investment efforts and work with professionals who truly have your interests at heart. The questions asked, concepts put forth, and definitions explained herein create a rudimentary road map to open your own door into the wealth management arena. They can arm you with helpful tools as you begin to apply financial strategies. Surround yourself with professionals who can ethically and morally serve your long-term financial needs, and you may better protect your retirement and other lifelong goals.

Wealth Management Industry Framework

The first chapter discusses figuring out the various paths to choose who to work with in the wealth management industry. Firm structures and professional organizations vary widely across the industry. Moreover, 95 percent of the general retail investing public do not monetarily qualify to be considered high-net-worth or institutional investors. If you fall into this 95 percent category, it is absolutely critical in the beginning stages of investment planning that you come to an understanding of the type of firm and financial advisor to suit your needs.

Too often, financial advisors will simply take on a client with a smaller account simply to pad their own book of business and show upper management that they are actively accumulating assets for the firm. However, what good will such advisors actually do for a client if their main goal is just to open the account, collect the assets, and then ignore investments and communications with clients? It happens more than anyone realizes. Unfortunately, this has become the standard operational method for many financial advisors as they seek to fulfill their asset quotas to retain their jobs with their current firms. Much of the blame for this can be laid at the heels of investment firms' upper-level executives. Those executives can pressure rank-and-file employees to produce ever-increasing margins that become unsustainable in the final analysis.

Your Financial Professional

Whether your financial advisor is a proactive money manager or just a middleman trying to collect assets is another imperative consideration. The type of advisor you work with has serious implications for your long-term personal savings success. You must also consider how to begin working with financial professionals by learning to discern which investment firm component is speaking to you. Subtle differences exist in realizing where the information you're being told comes from. In other words, an investor needs to discern between a financial advisor's actual convictions versus information being forced through that advisor by upper management. Compliance and legal departments of investment firms often prioritize their own protection and self-interest over the relationship between the client and financial advisor.

Internal Advisor Changes

Once you establish the right type of firm and advisor to entrust your money, the next thing to consider is the corporate internal change that may affect the client-advisor relationship over the long term. The winds of change can cut both ways. They can either help or harm the plan and strategy that you establish with your financial advisor. In this day and age, it is common for wealth managers, financial advisors, and insurance agents to move to other firms frequently. This has to do mainly with constant rotational changes made by upper management within brokerage firms or insurance agencies. It could affect or be related to advisor compensation, suitable investment product access, client fees, or legal liability, for example. An investor should always ask why the change was made when working with a financial advisor.

The importance of getting to the root and motivation for the change is paramount to protect your savings and legacy. If the motives for change are not fully brought to light then potential harm could be done to a retail investor. The investor might be unaware of what was occurring behind the curtain of the firm's operations. Other internal changes addressed involve many firms' common yet unethical practice of churning new brokers, the appropriate length of time for a financial advisor to be in the profession, and the regulatory broker protocol affecting an investor's wealth management plan.

Moral Investment Management, Not Just Ethical

Morality and money are two words that come into conflict with one another more often than not. Moral and biblical teachings are rife with examples of how the pursuit of wealth accumulation can interfere with personal or professional judgment; hence, the reason for this book's title being *Traps of Treasure*, with emphasis on the *traps*. You only need to look at major headlines any given year to see how easily the conflict arises. From televangelists funding lavish lifestyles using believers' donations to corporate titans using insider trading or creative accounting, the moral obligation to protect investors' money gets pushed aside and instead turns into a moral hazard.

Moral hazard shows up in the relentless effort by unethical professionals to put the money to use for purposes other than growing a client's assets and securing a sustainable future for them. Along these lines, the differentiation between discretionary versus nondiscretionary and fiduciary versus nonfiduciary is discussed. These terms may often be heard in television commercials or glossy advertising brochures. It is important to understand their application to the client-advisor relationship. Furthermore, it is important to understand that these terms represent more than marketing taglines used to reassure potential investors considering working with a firm.

Philosophical Strategies and Product Types

As an investor, you need to recognize where moral traps may pop up in your new relationship. To help in this recognition, it would be prudent to have a basic understanding of various financial strategy philosophies. Multiple approaches and a myriad of economic theories pervade the financial professions. Trying to understand the complex technical underpinnings of these ideologies can become all time consuming. A more effective approach would be to choose one or two methods for your investment strategy and then stick with it over time, even when your approach may not be in vogue or may be at the bottom of its cycle.

With greater focus on one or two methods, consistency through time can lead to greater odds of achieving your retirement goals and passing on a legacy to the next generation. Knowing what kind of financial advisor to work with has serious ramifications for your plan. For example, some advisors advocate investing with no short- or long-term changes to your investments. On the other hand, some advisors believe constant monitoring and actively rotating investments grow a portfolio more effectively. Similarly, the profession is filled with some advisors who take a very technical investing approach with all the meticulous calculating detail of an engineer. In contrast, other financial advisors prefer to study more the psychological trends of the economy to divine upcoming patterns.

In addition to the different philosophies practiced by advisors or firms, an investor should educate themselves on the endless buffet of available product types. Investment product availability will depend on whether the product is accessible to general retail investors or whether it is made accessible only to the upper ranks of the institutional investing world. For the most part, *Traps of Treasure* discusses methods and selections available to the general retail investors. The financial industry and regulatory environment put up numerous barriers and walls to the retail investing public. This is imposed so retail investors may not use products or features made available only to ultrahigh-net-worth individuals and those with access to the most elite personal relationships of financial and political circles. The morality of this is highly questionable and is a topic for a completely separate discussion not touched upon in *Traps of Treasure*. While the flaws of the larger financial system may not be able to be changed with quick or effective results, not all hope is lost for the retail investing public. With careful selection and vigilance, a novice investor can begin to see behind the curtains of investment firms and potentially dodge their roadblocks or traps.

Fraud and Proper Communication

A moral allegory heard by many is that it can often be easier for a camel to pass through the eye of a needle than it is for a rich person to enter the gates of paradise. In one sense, this story refers to the unnecessary accumulation of wealth through deceptive practices or evasive behavior. What is almost never seen by the investing public is the excessive amount of libel, slander, and fraudulent claims brought upon many financial advisors or investment firms. They commonly become subjects of fraudulent attacks by greedy attorneys seeking big payouts through unmeritorious settlements or false claims.

Financial advisor and investment firm reputations are often cloaked beneath private arbitration or employment agreements. Because of this, novice investors do not often see undercurrents that affect the decisions made for them by advisors and firm management. In other words, it is too easy for anyone or a specialized attorney to file false claims against an advisor or firm. Therefore, many advisors are left with no other choice but to guard themselves and remain silent on many issues out of fear of liability. In turn, perhaps this leaves the investor inadequately served, as the advisor or firm places their own protection against frivolous claims at the top of their priorities.

Sadly, the legal profession and immoral attorneys figured out how to game the financial industry to line their own pockets with proceeds from false claims against financial advisors and firms. An individual investor should ask their financial advisor if they work with clients or other professionals who could pose a liability risk to the advisor's own practice. An advisor who understands that having fewer high quality clients, as opposed to more clients who may pose risk, is worth his weight in gold to you as your advisor. Simply put, such an advisor prioritizes the long-term security and stability of his practice for his clients' interest and will better guide you to a solid foundation for years to come. It's a matter of quality over quantity when it comes to the size of a financial advisor's book of business.

Many financial advisors also attempt to limit communication with their clients to save their own time. They may also be worried about compliance interference in the relationship. When beginning to work with a financial advisor, it is critical to define the nature, preferred mode, and frequency of communication. Setting realistic and manageable expectations regarding communication cannot be overemphasized. How to communicate with an advisor and how to set expectations will also be discussed.

Fake News

What can one say about the media? Overused taglines, stale marketing gimmicks, and useless rhetoric populate the airwaves. Yet wasteful advertisement still exists and entire business models run their platforms on it across all sectors of the economy, including finance. The important thing for the novice investor to realize is that headlines constantly recreate and recycle daily to ensnare those who easily lose focus on goals. An investor needs to equip themselves with fortitude and perseverance to ignore the constant barrage of noise and clickbait in newspapers, websites, or television.

Constant media headline rotation, hearsay, conjecture, and embellishment psychologically compel people to take action so media outlets can glean money from the unsuspecting or uninformed. In reality, it is more prudent not to take compulsive action. The ability to recognize when you are succumbing to impulsive media influence redirects you back to your overall financial strategy and avoids useless distractions. Chasing the "hot dot" is never a wise path to take when making financial decisions. Nevertheless, it is human nature to be attracted to the trend or product of the day and the temptations of novelty. Learning how to spot trend manipulation and superfluous noise helps an investor avoid the media's trove of tactics. Doing so adds necessary discipline to a financial strategy.

Keeping Up with Your Peers

Aside from dodging the treacherous foils and traps of media deceit, a novice investor must also be aware of his or her relative standing within the investing world. Misunderstanding your portfolio's potential abilities can leave you with a negative, counterproductive sense of self. Time and time again, individuals obsess over their success or failure compared to neighbors, social groups, and professional colleagues. However, the only thing that truly matters when investing is accurate measuring of your own goals against your own abilities, location, and original goals.

We compare ourselves too often to others who have more than what we have or to unrealistic lifestyles portrayed by those living fabricated advertisements of a life. On the contrary, advertised lifestyles rarely come close to the reality of how the ultrahigh-net-worth individuals truly live with all their hidden problems and disguised agendas. Second-guessing our own circumstances ends up being a detriment to navigating the investment world. Therefore, it is imperative that a novice investor does not fall prey to keeping up with the Joneses. A better path to take would be to define highly specific, tangible, and realistic objectives over reasonable time frames and not to stray from that vision. Targeted focus on your vision while ignoring external distractions increases odds that you will reach your envisioned lifestyle and financial security.

Reinventing the Wheel

The last critical topic addressed in *Traps of Treasure* is the nature by which investment firms reinvent themselves. Branding, organizational structure, and strategies to tackle fading interest are among the tools used. Long-term detailed memory frequently gets lost on the investing public from decade to decade. Through that loss, financial institutions play shell games by switching products or personnel in and out of favor. From the investor's perspective, it is important to stay abreast of industry changes. Strategies that were once in vogue become outdated and ineffective through the years. The resulting stagnation of an investor's portfolio can often be prevented with diligent attention throughout the client-advisor working relationship.

After addressing the above topics throughout the book, a final bulleted summary outlines a preliminary path to begin your search to work with the right advisor for your needs. The bullet points provide step-by-step considerations to ponder as you start building your wealth legacy. Additionally, the book provides appendices of investment product types and questions a new investor should ask of their chosen advisor or firm.

Nothing less than absolute clarity about the advisor's positions should be expected. Any attempt to evade a question or give an indeterminate answer should be a glaring red flag that a client's interests may not be served there. How the advisor or firm responds to the questions will inform your decision. It will shed light on whether they are truly there to help guide you or whether they primarily exist to enrich themselves by just adding more new clients.

As we dive into the detailed topics of *Traps of Treasure*, bear in mind that the ability to see clearly through investment firm dynamics, edifices, and relationships could possibly be the greatest skill an investor can equip themselves with. Doing so could protect an investor's financial future and minimize disruptions to a lifelong plan of saving for a solid and peaceful retirement. Having faith in your financial advisor and trusting the investment firm does not mean walking blindly through your endeavors in finance. Constant vigilance to the inner workings and conflicts within firms is mandatory to set your financial strategy on a successful path.

When you achieve the clarity of vision needed to see through the many games or sleights of hand within the investment industry then can you begin to have trust. Faith will build thereafter with your advisors as they help guide you ethically, morally, and satisfactorily to a sound and stable financial life in the long run. Remember, constant skepticism in believing what you see or hear regarding anything related to investing is the saving grace that just may help prevent you from being taken advantage of. You'll be able to sleep better at night once you are able to cut through the hype and false promises permeating the investment world. With the myriad of ways investment marketing and media propaganda attempt to dupe the general investing public, always realize that what you see is rarely what you get in what can often be an unethical game of bait and switch from the less moral players of the financial world.

CHAPTER 1

The Road to Damascus
Figuring Out Your Path

So where do you begin? With an endless array of options to choose from in the investing world, the first critical step is to see through the common taglines and repetitive jargon. Saul was blinded by the light of the Divine to see his true path. Sometimes it takes an unpleasant experience to open your eyes and discover the correct path to travel. Initially, Saul was self-assured in his purpose and methods. Yet only after God blinded him did he see what his true purpose entailed. At that point, Saul finally decided to discard his former misconceptions. Saul's following transformation and struggles led him to his own conversion to the truth. Thereafter, he eventually became the person we know him by today, Saint Paul.

Similarly, market propaganda and commercials blind us by making us indifferent to the actual truth of what happens within the investing world. To correctly find your path, an investor must recognize the differences among the investment firm structures and their different functions. The structure of the firm can have serious implications for your savings' long-term growth. Not all firms and financial advisors are organized to put the interest of the investor first. Nevertheless, many firms may still disseminate seductive but misleading advertisement through various channels. Let's begin our look into deciding your proper path by explaining the various types of investment firms.

Independent Broker, Wire House, RIA, or DIY

For the general retail investor who wants to begin saving for retirement, four main options exist. They are (1) the independent broker, (2) the large wire house firm, (3) the RIA or registered investment advisor, and (4) the DIY or do-it-yourself online trading platforms. As a private wealth manager, I have worked with or under each of these four investment platform categories. In my experience, I have found the independent broker to offer the greatest benefit to the retail investor.

The independent broker

The independent broker usually structures itself in a way where its financial advisors are less beholden to the dictates of upper management. Financial advisors who affiliate with independent brokerages generally have more freedom to select products. They also typically find themselves under less pressure to meet production quotas that large wire houses or global banks may impose upon their advisors. This leads to a significant benefit for the investor.

First, with smaller or no production quotas, your financial advisor will be less conflicted. Because the advisor feels less pressured, he will be able to focus impartially toward your financial strategy. He will be less likely to be under constant pressure to sell you products that may not align with your intended portfolio allocation. More often than not, I have seen too many advisors use heavy-handed sales tactics upon their clients with products that are untested, too risky, or too conservative for the client's needs. Most of the time, this is the result of high-pressure directives or job-loss threats coming from upper level or C-Suite executives within a firm.

There's an unspoken reality about such situations within many larger firms. Their top brass allow the desire for forced or unsustainable bottom-line growth to interfere with what should be their main purpose. That main purpose should be to protect and provide for the growth of an investor's assets and comprehensive portfolio. Sadly, many firms lose sight of this purpose. In the absence of high-pressure sales tactics and quotas, the independent broker tends to more easily seek out what is best for the client as opposed to what the firm wants him to sell to meet corporate targets.

Next, independent brokerage firms and their advisors tend to operate on a more regional or local scale. Because they are smaller in size by assets, the reach of these firms rarely draws as much attention as the larger banks and wire houses that have extensive advertising budgets with national reach. The independent brokerage could be a simple structure of a lone financial advisor practicing solely by himself. But usually, the firms range in size from a couple dozen advisors and support staff to a midsize firm with several hundred advisors and staff to handle operations. Midsize firms tend to have their advisors congregate regionally or else the total number of advisors spread out thinly across the expanse of the nation.

Because of this spread, independent brokers garner less attention from the general investing public. Yet despite their lack of conspicuousness, they have much to offer in the way of better one-on-one personal service. Sometimes they can offer lower fees. Without massive advertising budgets, large quantities of legal personnel, or exorbitant executive salaries to support, the independent brokerage can many times offer the same or better quality of financial service at a lower price.

When I ask a new acquaintance why they choose to do business with their current financial professionals, I usually receive one of two replies. One is that they heard about their current financial professionals through a friend. The other is that they were impressed by the "security" offered by their current firm, as seen by advertisements and name recognition. However, there is flawed logic in assuming that following the herd can ensure security. As with the buffalo, the herd can many times be headed off a cliff together while each member is unaware of that fact. The general impression that sheer employee numbers or firm size can offer security is a blatant myth that should not be given any credibility. Therefore, it is critical when deciding who to work with not to discount smaller firms or individual advisors simply because they do not affiliate with one of the largest firms around.

Remember, many firm collapses and investor losses occurred under the custodianship of some of the most storied and largest firms in the nation as we saw in the financial crisis of 2008 and during many market crashes or panics of past decades. How well did the resources and financial clout of those larger firms serve their clients? The answer is not at all. Essentially, the independent broker, while perhaps less glamorous or less visible, may provide greater objectivity than other firm structures.

With today's market interconnectedness and web communication, independent advisors have a much easier time connecting with people who may not have been within their geographical reach. Independent brokerages in past decades tended to focus their efforts and relationships locally. However, the speed and ease with which business can be transacted today makes working with an independent broker a much more viable option.

The wire house

In direct contrast to the independent broker, the wire house tends to be a very large brokerage house or bank with enormous resources to reach and attract the widest net of potential clients. These firms are the names you often hear in national television commercials. They typically employ thousands of advisors across the nation or even globally with total personnel counts running into the tens of thousands. Their far-reaching scope and total supporting firm capital offers several advantages. But many more pitfalls arise when dealing with such large firms.

Traps of Treasure focuses mainly on the retail investor and those who may not have enough saved to qualify as a primary client focus of the larger wire houses. For example, if a client does not have at least $500,000 to invest, many of the larger wire houses may reject an investor simply because the wire house and its advisors do not warrant such investors worth their time. More likely, the wire house may open an account with lesser funds but relegate it to support staff or a small department of low priority within the firm. As is often practiced, but rarely admitted, many times, wire house advisors simply want to catch their big fish to garnish annual fees based on the largest account size with the least effort.

Within the broader financial community, investors and clients tend to be grouped into general categories. *Accredited investors* or *qualified investors* are two terms often thrown around by larger firms internally to differentiate who they want to serve as clients. The $500,000 or above investment mark tends to be a common threshold where wire houses will be more than happy to accept you as a client and offer you preferential treatment. Further thresholds occur at several million dollars for high-net-worth investors and eventually on to the ultrahigh-net-worth investors with multimillion-dollar savings with room to spare. What relevance do these thresholds have to the Main Streeter or retail investors with less than those thresholds? The relevance lies in the impact upon savers' accounts via access to product types or attention to detail through comprehensive financial plans.

One little deceptive practice by the wire houses lies in their lack of transparency and truthfulness regarding available products. The probability of the matter is that some investment products and vehicles perform faster or with greater performance than others. Differentiation among products and how they are structured is intentional. Too many times we have heard that Wall Street continues to do well while Main Street gets left behind. This is not coincidence or merely luck on the part of Wall Street.

By separating out institutional from retail investors, the powers that be on Wall Street and those with significant regulatory clout create two separate classes whereby one class, the institutional, reaps the rewards of the most advanced structured products and garnishes the most financial gains. On the other hand, more mundane or lower-performing products are reserved for easy access by retail investors. Product performance for retail investors may remain lackluster over the long haul and impede significant growth of an investor's accounts.

Another small ruse used by the larger wire houses and reinforced by regulators lies in their justification for differentiating these two classes of investors. Claims will be made that it is for the protection of the retail or smaller investor. This is often used as the generalized justification why retail investors should not have access to the more advanced structured products or account types. However, if a client works with an advisor, the advisor would and should know the intricacies of such advanced products through the advisor's own research. Therefore, the client should at least have the ability to access such products if the client and individual advisor agree they could be beneficial to a client's portfolio. In other words, decisions about product type and usage should be made at the nearest professional relationship to the client, which is not always the case.

In reality, such decisions can be made by the highest levels of a wire house's compliance or legal department. The department can then mandate to the firm's advisors which directives and products must be followed or restricted under threat of being fired. Another reason why larger wire houses may not allow retail investors access to beneficial products could simply have to do with paperwork. If the masses of retail investors had access to the most advanced product types, this would create significantly more administrative work for the wire house. It could involve extensive paperwork, regulatory coordination, or legal liability. An investor must ask, Whose interests are being served by not allowing retail investors access to the most advanced products? The answer is the wire house's interests are served first; then perhaps the investor's interests can take secondary consideration.

By no means do I advocate that any retail investor should pursue advanced investment products without having thorough knowledge and performed adequate research of how those products work. But I do argue that retail investors should at least be given the option to pursue them without restriction or impediment if they choose in conjunction with their financial advisor or insurance agent. When deciding your path of who and what firm type to work with, it is better to be reassured that you will have access to every product type offered by that firm. It would be prudent to obtain a list from each firm of which products they offer and do a side-by-side comparison. That way, even if you do not intend to use many of the products or are unsure how they work, you will at least know you have options to choose them if future circumstances dictate a modification.

Despite all the potential pitfalls, there are certain areas where the major wire houses excel and can offer some benefit. Technology can be one of those areas where the large wire houses offer benefits. You may seek to have many different asset types integrated across accounts or portfolios. Sometimes it is easier to work with a large wire house in this scenario. The back-office and integrated platform support often provide easy-to-view big picture snapshots of an investor's overall assets.

Response times to questions or issues when working with a large wire house may or may not be better than working with an independent broker. In my experience, I have found that response time simply comes down to your chosen financial advisor or who is recommended to you. Not all advisors are created equal. Some will be perpetually motivated to move with all haste and move the world for you while others will put tasks on the backburner to play golf or give more time to their largest clients. This is an area where personality types and communication frequency expectations become critical to understand.

If you do decide to entrust your savings and hard-earned wealth to a wire house, a good place to start to protect yourself from the many traps they offer is to interrogate the firm with the questions provided at the end of this book in appendix B. By using the provided questions, a new investor may be armed with the necessary tools to see if the wire house can be direct and straightforward. Lack of clarity, hesitation, or inability to answer any of the appendix questions should be glaring red flags to the investor, signaling that perhaps this wire house or large bank does not hold the client's interests as top priority.

RIA (registered investment advisor)

Outside of the realm of independent brokers and wire houses is the registered investment advisor, or RIA, as an acronym. On the most basic level, what differentiates RIAs from the other two structures has to do with regulatory agencies and the collection of compensation. The two major regulatory agencies governing the financial advisory and wealth management professions are the Financial Industry Regulatory Authority (FINRA) and the Securities and Exchange Commission (SEC). Most of the general public is familiar with the SEC, at least by name, from having heard about it in the news and media productions. FINRA, on the other hand, was created in 2007 as a private entity to handle enforcement, arbitration, and regulation of members.

RIAs fall under the jurisdiction of the SEC, whereas brokerage firms typically fall under the jurisdiction of FINRA. An entire book could be written about the different functions between FINRA and the SEC. However, for this book's purposes and to keep terms on the simplest level for beginning investors, I will keep the explanation of the difference between the two limited to how fees and compensation are structured.

Compensation to brokers and their firms generally falls under two categories, commission based or fee based. Brokers and firms that charge commissions for each trade or transaction performed in an account are typically governed by FINRA. Brokers and firms that charge one annual fee, or a single fee spread out across several payments throughout the year, are typically governed by the SEC. Independent brokers and large wire houses many times offer both categories under one roof in what is called a hybrid structure. However, RIAs operate strictly as fee-based advisors under the SEC. This has one distinct advantage when it comes to conflict of interest in how compensation is paid to a firm or its advisors. When commissions are charged per trade or transaction, the individual payments to the broker or firm add up.

If you are unfortunate to be working with an unethical advisor, that advisor will increase the number of trades within a client's account to increase his or her overall pay. Whether it is done with or without the client's consent, this is a practice known as churning, which is illegal. The advantage of working with an RIA is that the RIA cannot charge individual transaction commissions. By fixing compensation as an annual percentage of the assets managed, the RIA has no motivation to increase or manipulate the number of trades performed in a client's account over time. Therefore, the RIA is more likely to focus efforts on what strategies will work best for a client as opposed to how much money they can make from churning trades.

To further explain structures of an RIA, it is important to understand that independent brokers and wire houses can each choose to offer RIA services and be regulated under the SEC to offer fee-based services. Or they can choose to structure themselves solely as broker dealers who charge commissions regulated under FINRA. There are a myriad of combinations that financial advisors and financial services firms can choose from to structure their offerings and compensation structure to the general public.

What's important to know is that RIAs provide fee-based services, which helps to avoid the conflict of interest that commission-based compensation may present. RIA is a rather large umbrella term that encompasses a large swath of financial firms. An RIA can be a single individual advisor operating a sole practitioner wealth management practice from his home office, all the way up to the largest banks and wealth management firms on the planet. If you want to know if the financial professional you are considering working with is an RIA or an investment advisor representative who works within an RIA, you can simply go to the SEC's website to search for their name and learn about their registration history.

DIY (do-it-yourself)

The last of the four main categories on the road to investing is the do-it-yourself platform. These platforms and firm structures are the financial service providers who often advertise no- or low-commission trading through their online trading platforms. Such platforms are rather seductive because they allow the investor to feel as if they have a sense of control over the minute aspects of their trading accounts. Engineers, retired investors, and those with highly technical mindsets often like such platforms out of self-interest to stay engaged with the investing world as opposed to handing their money to someone else to manage. While the do-it-yourself platforms are engaging and informative, they provide many pitfalls and negative outcomes for investors explained as follows.

One thing that do-it-yourself online trading platforms offer, which is very enticing, is the option to trade for your own account without having to pay commissions or fees. While that seems very alluring, the old adage that "nothing comes for free" could never be truer. If the online trading platforms are not making money by charging you any commissions or fees, then how can they afford to stay in business to operate? The answer is that you, the investor, with your account on their platform, is their product by which they accumulate funds among institutions. Many of these online platforms boast in their national advertising that they are the largest or one of the largest custodians of retirement savers' funds in the nation.

What is not seen is that such platforms need to amass such large quantities of investors' funds in order to use the collective critical mass of those funds for overnight funds trading. This a complex area of institutional investing that retail investors do not encounter. But suffice it to say, the funds you invest in an account with online do-it-yourself platforms are being used to generate revenue for those platforms, just not in the way that the average investor can imagine or visibly see. The bottom line is, if they're not selling you anything so they can make a fee or commission, then you yourself are the product being sold.

Another pitfall of the do-it-yourself platforms is the lack of personal support when problems or technical issues arise. Assuming that you become knowledgeable enough to navigate the trading desk and internal sections of an online trading platform, there still lie problems with how the help desk of these platforms operate. The so-called support staff, designated advisor, or help desk are usually salaried employees who need to meet targets mandated by their corporate overlords. The less time they speak with you on the phone and the higher number of new accounts they open, the better for them. Having used such platforms myself before I entered the financial services field and became a wealth manager, I experienced all too often the disturbing behavior of being put on hold or transferred through an endless array of call-line options only to be left with no suitable answer or resolution to my questions and issues a half hour later.

Similarly, if an online platform's help line personnel detect, in any way or form, that the client is preparing to leave the platform, the personnel will immediately direct the caller to another "specialist" on another line whose sole purpose is to convince and coerce the caller to retain their investments with that company. Sadly, the business models of many of these do-it-yourself platforms focus solely on servicing the firm at the expense of the client, in both time and money. Adding to the frustration of inadequate personal service from their support staff, do-it-yourself platforms often offer robo-advisor or preconstructed portfolios. These options are used by the platforms as a quick tool to keep unknowing investors under the mindset that their funds and investments are properly allocated or protected.

Any financial advisor or wealth manager with even half their wits about them understands that such automated investment allocations cannot adequately address the unique needs of every investor. Yet these options are advertised and pushed upon new investors. Why? Simply because giving investors on their platforms a false sense of security allows the platforms and their employees to save time. This saved time is then devoted to the never-ending cycle of pitching to new prospects so they can be brought on board, hence, adding to the overall assets managed by these platforms.

A proper and suitable investment strategy, financial plan, or portfolio allocation should be constructed with the necessary attention to detail based upon a client's actual changing life situations. Platitudes, feel-good commercials, and cookie-cutter investment allocation approaches cannot sufficiently address clients' needs to create a well-constructed long-term plan. In order to achieve a successful plan, one of the other three main category options are most likely a better fit for someone who is a beginner on their route to investing or saving for retirement.

The great irony about do-it-yourself online trading platforms is that they market their services toward the very people who are least likely to reap the benefits of such platforms. Many beginning investors are attracted to the option to be able to trade or invest without having to pay any fees or commissions. However, it's often said that you get what you pay for. Successful investing or planning for retirement requires not only having a good grasp of the technical side of trading on a platform but also a well-honed sense of the psychology of the markets, the cycles or undercurrents that run through economic cycles, and the various complicated product structures that exist throughout capital markets.

All in all, do-it-yourself platforms are probably most suitable for professionals who have already had an extensive career in the financial field or are retired and need a platform to use for their continued personal trading. I would not suggest that any novice investor engage these platforms until they have attained a broader understanding of the markets after years of continuous and disciplined trading. If you are tempted to try your skills by opening up an account for yourself on one of these platforms, then, by all means, have fun and good luck. But don't be surprised when you can't understand why your hard-earned funds have diminished over time while you can't put a specific pinpoint as to why.

Having covered the four main categories of investment firm organizational structures, it is important to emphasize and have a clear understanding of the motives and operational patterns within each. Comprehending how and why these different types of firms behave the way they do will help to inform you of which type of structure is appropriate for you to choose. Starting down the road of your investment future is a daunting task with far too many options available before your eyes. It is too easy to be led down the wrong path by unethical marketing practices or incomplete solicitation pitches that do not tell the whole story of how you will be treated as a client.

By the time Saul had his vision corrected through the grace of God, too much damage had been done in previous years. And while he was able to redeem himself, each novice investor should start by asking themselves one critical question: Will choosing this path for my financial future with this advisor and firm lead me down a path of sustainable growth and success, or will it lead me to a pattern of being stuck on a wheel that doesn't stop turning? Discerning for yourself if the path that others will lead you down is the right path is perhaps the most invaluable decision a new investor can make. In the long run, choosing the right path can help you avoid the immoral or deceptive practices to which many clients fall prey.

Money Manager or Middleman—Which Kind of Advisor Do You Have?

Now that we have a basic understanding of the various brokerage or platform structures, the next critical assessment to make is understanding the individual you work with and choose to help guide you through your investing and saving years. Within the structure of each of the four types of platforms just discussed, it is important to specifically understand exactly who you are dealing with when you hire a financial professional. Even if you are the type of person who likes to invest for yourself on an online trading platform, you will encounter numerous people within a firm or corporation all vying for your attention and your monetary assets.

Financial advisor, financial planner, private wealth manager, financial consultant, and broker—these are often interchangeable terms describing the same role. Different firms will use the titles in different fashions. And there will usually be an array of fancy acronyms after a financial professional's official designation. Of course, all these titles and credentials are nice to see to inform an investor that the professional has been through and passed the requisite licensing qualifications for their role.

However, one thing I've learned in my years within the financial profession is that one concept supersedes any title, certification, degree, or acronym. That concept has to do with understanding whether the professional you work with is actually a money manager or if he or she is simply the middleman who gathers your account for a firm and then passes the nitty-gritty work of creating your portfolio and allocation to someone else, such as a specialist within a firm or an independent third-party money manager.

Defining the money manager

Delving into the terminology of the money manager requires a long discussion of the many different regulatory and designation qualifications required of money managers. For instance, many money managers are required to submit regulatory reports to the SEC on a quarterly basis to show the actual holdings and trading patterns within their funds. However, for the purpose of this book and to keep the discussion on a simpler level, we will not give detailed explanations of all the possible functions of money managers. For our purposes, we will use the term on a more generalized level to define a financial professional who takes the time his or herself to actually research, select, and implement the actual individual products and positions that make up your investment portfolio. In contrast, we will use the term *middleman* here in the book to define a financial professional who does not perform the aforementioned functions but instead serves the role within a financial firm of bringing new assets and clients under the firm's umbrella or on their platform.

The reason that understanding this difference is so important is because it has significant impact on the long-term costs of investing with a specific advisor or brokerage firm. The concept of the actual money manager has become a downplayed role in recent decades within the larger wire houses and even some larger independent brokerages. Decades ago, it was commonplace to have the individual advisor or wealth manager a client works with do all the actual trades and product selection for each client's account. However, as business models changed and larger firms found ways to increase growth and productivity, many financial advisors simply became asset gatherers, where their role became relegated to merely bringing new client relationships to a firm and more money under the firm's custodianship. And while these advisors still retain all the same licensure credentials, they effectively have become middlemen who charge a fee or commission added on top of the independent money managers who actually perform the detailed functions of selecting investments and planning out buy-or-sell trading patterns.

Internally, within many firms, pressure comes from higher level executives down to the ground troops of a firm's financial advisor team. Those hidden internal directives pressure individual financial advisors to only focus on gathering new clients and new relationships. Once a new relationship is acquired, the advisor is expected to pass the detailed work of account allocation to another team within the firm. This kind of relationship with your new advisor then simply becomes one of you talking to a go-between salesman.

Large firms have found that this relationship structure serves greater profits for the firm. Yet it leaves the client one more degree detached from the actual mechanics of how their money is invested. Sadly, this was not always the way it was. But as the decades passed from the sixties, seventies, eighties, or even as recent at the nineties, the business models changed and moved away from individual customization for every single client. Nowadays, such individualized portfolio customization and attention is usually only reserved for the ultrahigh-net-worth individuals or families who can offer a firm the greatest amount of annual fees based on the proportional size of their holdings with the firm.

One way around this dilemma for a new investor would be to simply ask and hold accountable a prospective advisor they may work with, whether that advisor will actually be doing the trading and selection of investments for the account. If the advisor comes back with glossy brochures or long-winded explanations of how they can provide a great selection of third-party money managers or internal portfolio managers either within or outside their firm, the odds are you are most likely speaking to a middleman and not someone who will give you the detailed attention your hard-earned savings deserve.

The middleman passing game

It is becoming rarer to find a financial advisor or wealth manager who is still willing to manage every minute detail of a client's portfolio. But they do still exist. You just have to ask the specific questions about how investments and products will be selected and by whom. Most firms will argue that, by using choice independent money managers, they are doing their due diligence and performing their duties to you as a client. The problem is, though, that multiple layers of money managers or third-party managers can obscure the view of what is actually occurring within your portfolio. It's a method of smoke and mirrors that allows large firms to present an illusion of responsibility to the client, when in reality, it simply makes things harder to get to the root of the construction of your savings and where your money is going.

This is not to say that independent or third-party money managers are not useful. Many of them have excellent performance track records and can be trusted with investors' savings. The problem lies in the client's detachment from knowing exactly what is going into their accounts and where their money is being placed. For this reason, it is critical to differentiate whether the advisor or broker you choose is hands on enough and willing to the do the detailed work of a money manager for you.

Costs of a money manager or middleman

Cost comes into play through the selection of money managers as well. Companies of money managers whose sole function is to create funds or portfolios for mass distribution and purchase in client accounts will charge a fee on top of what your financial advisor already charges. Therefore, in essence, you could be paying layers of fees on an annual basis without even knowing it if you, as a client, are not aware of what is in your accounts. Some money manager fees can be exorbitant relative to the provided annual performance. Being ever vigilant to the nested layers of managers and fees being used within your investment portfolio can help you to recognize unnecessary fees being charged to your accounts.

By efficiently reducing the overall fees or commissions to your accounts, the added money can compound through the years to help grow your savings even further. Choosing the advisor or broker who still serves the function of money manager, as opposed to the more common role of middleman that most advisors become pigeonholed into these days within their firms, will help to bring you one step closer to understanding what the nature of your investments are and how they are being appropriated.

The Puppet or the Ventriloquist: Client Facing or Back Office—Know Who Is Speaking to You

For the last segment of this chapter, as we look within the structures of firm types and their internal advisors, we should also discuss knowing who is truly speaking to you as you speak with your financial professional. Many times, your financial advisor or wealth manager will be thinking one thing in his true convictions. Yet the directives brought down upon advisors within many large firms often prevent them from saying what they truly think. This form of muzzling occurs more often than anyone suspects. The source of such directives could be coming from a firm's legal department or compliance department.

Another scenario involves branch or regional managers who are more interested in protecting their turf and expect their team of advisors to toe the line specific to the manager's agenda. In other words, it is important to discern whether what your advisor tells you is what's most beneficial for your savings strategy or it if came down from a higher or related source that is thinking only of guarding the firm's interests and profits before the client's. Therefore, in a sense, your financial advisor may be forced into the role of being just a puppet who is unfortunately constrained to repeating the refrains of upper management or back-office personnel. At the same time, the management or back-office personnel effectively play to the role of puppet master or ventriloquist to push their directives through the communications clients hear from their advisor.

The back office

The back office of a firm usually comprises administrative, legal, compliance, management, HR, and other departments, which, in their specialized functions, are supposed to support a financial advisor's day-to-day running of their practice. Depending upon the firm or brokerage you do business with, the effect these departments can have on a financial advisor vary widely among firms. Some firms will be extremely forceful and pressure their advisors to put forth certain messages, while other firms, usually the independent brokerages, will often give more space to their advisors to run their practices in the manner they see fit within the confines of laws and regulations. Several examples are offered here to explain some instances of how larger firms can control the message that a client receives from their advisor.

One instance to be wary of is meeting with a new advisor who claims that their firm can offer you a completely open platform of products and services. *Open platform* is a term intended to describe the ability of a firm to offer an unlimited array of products available on the market without restrictions, unless they are the most advanced type of structured products. Many times, this *open platform* phrase is a tagline used to make prospective clients believe that they will be able to invest in whatever type of product they choose.

After choosing a firm, however, it often sinks in and becomes reality that the advisor will admit after the fact that they are not able to put certain products in a client's account when the client asks. The reason for this could be many, but most often, it has to do with the existing relationships between the brokerage firm and the product companies. By limiting the types of products or companies to choose from in your portfolio, the firm could be doing you a disservice and possibly preventing you from utilizing certain products that could add more growth to your investments. Customarily, the firm and its financial advisors also may not provide recommendations on company products that they do not have custody or hold in-house themselves due to lack of an existing relationship.

Another instance that most clients may not be aware of is the effect compliance departments have upon financial advisors. Given the litigious nature of society, most financial firms and brokerages take an extremely conservative line when it comes to adhering to every minute detail of protocol. This can cause a firm to be afraid of their own shadow, so to speak, and impose strict penalties upon advisors who don't maintain the utmost code of silence outside of the minimum required communications with clients.

At best, the client is left to have to probe and do their own research to discover if they are being told adequate information to serve their savings and retirement purposes. What's worse is that most clients don't even know what questions to ask if they don't have much experience in the realm of finances. The only true way for a client to circumvent this conundrum is to ask the exact same questions, word for word, without variation, of different advisors or different firms and compare the resultant answers. By fielding enough answers from several distinct sources, the bigger picture of correct answers can come into focus.

Product peddling

And the last instance of back-office control of advisors relates to pushing certain types of products. Even if the firm is a truly open platform with many choices, that does not mean the firm does not pressure its advisors to sell the firm's own proprietary products. Those proprietary products are the internal constructs of the firm and may or may not be suitable products for investors. Prime examples of this were the collateralized debt obligations (CDOs) and collateralized mortgage obligations (CMOs) that contributed to the collapse of the housing market and created the financial crisis of 2008. Any investor should be skeptical of any product created by the firm they currently custody their assets with. After all, large wire houses and brokerage firms are in the business to make money, many times at any cost without regard to the safety or reliability of the investment products they create.

In my own experience, I have been fortunate enough, regardless of how I structured my practice or which firm I was with, that I was never pressured by management to sell specific products. Nevertheless, my experience as a wealth manager is more an exception than the rule. The majority of advisors and wealth managers do succumb to the pressures of selling certain products pushed by upper management at large firms. Choosing to do business with an independent broker or firm will, generally speaking, reduce the odds that such product pressure tactics will be used upon you as a client.

It can often be hard to tell which component of a firm is speaking to you—your financial advisor or the management of a firm. But with frequent contact with your financial professional, meaning several times per year at least, you should be able to start to detect personality traits or hesitation in the advisor's responses. This will help you know when your advisor may be contemplating what the ventriloquists are directing him or her to say as opposed to what he or she would like to tell you.

Altogether, figuring out your path of which firm or advisor to work with, recognizing the true money managers from the middlemen, and honing your skill to detect when your advisor is telling you something perhaps different from his true convictions are the primary steps as you begin to delve into the investing world. Understanding what happens between the internal relationships of financial advisors and their companies is another avenue to investigate to help you and is addressed in the next chapter.

CHAPTER 2

Winds of Change
When Change Can Help or Harm

What has become standard practice in the wealth management industry is the frequent relocation of advisors to other firms. As you start on your journey to invest, the ideal situation for any new investor would be to find a professional who they could consistently remain with over decades throughout the entire course of their investing lives. However, the structure of the wealth management profession and many other factors often make such a possibility a rare occurrence.

Perhaps the few exceptions to this are the highest-net-worth family offices and trusts that are custodied or domiciled within countries or financial institutions that root themselves in lack of change. Such institutions can be hard to find for the everyday Main Streeter and retail investor. So what is a new client to do? Several behaviors of financial professionals and firms should come to light and be the forefront of any investor's search process. These practices include understanding when and why financial advisors will change firms and also recognizing when a brokerage firm is using the pump-and-dump scheme of young new advisors simply to acquire mores assets for the firm's book of business.

Separately, it is helpful to know what appropriate lengths of time a financial advisor or private wealth manager should remain at a firm or how long they have been in the business. This can help inform you if the advisor will be stable enough to provide you with long-term consistent managerial advice over your portfolio. The last issue, which is a very critical one addressed in this chapter, is a regulation known as the broker protocol. This protocol can have significant impact on you as an individual investor because it has the potential to interfere with your personal relationship with your financial advisor.

Essentially, the protocol addresses and governs a financial advisor's relationship with brokerage firms and often dictates how or when a financial advisor may be allowed to associate with specific firms. Taken together, all these considerations can guide you to know when you, as a client, may need to make a change yourself regarding the relationships you have, either with your financial professional or a specific brokerage firm.

Musical Brokers

When the time comes for financial advisors to change firms, a client should ask themselves many questions regarding whether they should follow the advisor with their accounts to the advisor's new firm or whether they should remain loyal to the current custodian firm. A client's answer should depend on the motives and influences that prompted the move by the advisor. Over the course of my career, I myself have affiliated with several firms, each of which were appropriate to my career level and needs to fulfill certain client obligations at those respective times.

In my own experience and in my own opinion, I found that structuring my own wealth management practice under a hybrid and independent RIA brokerage firm allowed me to serve my clients with the greatest flexibility and least impediment to offering my client's purely objective market assessments. While other advisors will disagree with me, I am firm in my conviction that the manner in which I structure my practice allows me to put my clients' concerns far above any marketing, commission, fee, or regulatory worries. But aside from my own practice, let's take a look at what may invoke a transition by a financial advisor.

TRAPS OF TREASURE

Payout structures

The most obvious matter at stake that could affect the client-advisor-firm relationship would be the compensation to the advisor. Some people among the general public have a vague understanding that financial advisors get paid either by receiving a commission for every trade they perform or else by receiving a small percentage of a portfolio's total value on an annual basis. While commissions vary from firm to firm, a fee-based advisor generally makes anywhere from 1 percent to 2 percent per year of an account's total value per year. This is standard practice across the industry. However, what many investors do not understand is the amount of money that the firm keeps of an advisor's commissions or fees.

The brokerage firm's cut of the fees, if the advisor is not structured as a solely independent RIA himself, typically range anywhere from 10 percent to 70 percent. As you can see, there is a huge disparity there. So if your advisor is unfortunate enough to be working for a brokerage firm or wire house that takes seventy cents of every dollar he makes, odds are that your advisor may be more worried about asset production since he will always have to keep obtaining more assets under management just to keep up with the firm's voracious expenditure appetite. Where does that 70 percent cut go? Well, that cut often funds the many back-office departments, legal teams, marketing teams, office rentals, and upper-level management salaries of large firms with enormous overhead.

On the other hand, many advisors choose to structure themselves independently. By doing so, many independent brokerage firms will only take roughly 10 percent to 20 percent of an advisor's fee or commission production. Therefore, the advisor will be allowed to retain greater pay based on invested time and effort per client or household. It stands to reason that when your financial advisor is happy with take-home pay, he will most likely be more motivated to put in the extra effort and give greater detailed attention to your portfolio or financial plan. Simply put, it benefits a client or investor to understand the pay structure that a financial advisor works under.

The payout structures are not data that a financial advisor is freely allowed to discuss with clients due to internal information restrictions imposed by many firms. So while a financial advisor may not be able to disclose his payout structure he receives from the firm, it would behoove an investor to inquire of and press branch managers or upper-level management of a brokerage firm to precisely explain how much take-home pay the advisors of a firm receive of their total production. If the upper-level management is not willing to answer or offers a vague explanation, chances are the advisors are not receiving as much pay as they could be under other brokerage firms' payout structures.

Overbearing compliance

Another reason why a financial advisor may leave a firm could have to do with heavy-handed compliance restrictions or restrictions on communications. Under current regulatory regimes, financial advisors and wealth managers are severely restricted in how they can communicate with clients. Due to an egregious number of regulations and potential traps for advisors, social media presences, telephone communication lines, marketing material, and even seminars are all controlled with an iron-fisted grip. The number of loopholes that a financial advisor must go through to receive approval for any printed form of communication, along with the potential for rejection of those communications, makes developing outward-facing communications with the public extremely burdensome and time consuming. Therefore, many advisors simply reduce the amount of regular communication they have with the public due to the hassle.

Where it affects a client is in receiving adequate and consistent communication from your financial advisor. Depending upon the firm your advisor is with, some advisors are so restricted and under threat of penalty from their firm for making even the slightest recommendation that they effectively become too afraid of their own shadow to tell you what is really on their mind. In contrast, some advisor's firms and compliance departments allow them to create their own published material with greater ease. Depending upon how restrictive your advisor's compliance department is, the relationship between you and your advisor can be materially different in nature and personality. In my opinion, it is more productive for an investor to find an advisor whose firm will allow them to communicate freely through published means, whether those publishings be of a social media, printed article, seminar, webinar, brochure, or any other form of material marketing aside from phone conversations.

Client poachers

Poaching of clients from advisors or succession issues within a brokerage firm can also bear weight with an advisor influencing whether he remains with a firm or not. For instance, some more unethical advisors or ones with many more years' experience than a younger advisor may find an opening in conversation or social gatherings to interject themselves into another advisor's prospective relationships. Through this interjection, they then effectively usurp the relationship and materially retain the prospect as a client for themselves, when in reality, the advisor who was the original communicator loses the relationship. This situation can happen from time to time among advisors grouped closely together within larger firms. If it does, the advisor who lost out on the relationship due to the unethical advisor could become demoralized since assets that should have been his to manage effectively go to a relationship parasite who is trying to steal other's relationships to pad their book of business.

As well, sometimes advisors have carrots dangled in front of their face by upper management promising them the succession to an older advisor's book of business. This is a common trick used by many managerial professionals in the wealth management industry to ensure that younger advisors, and hence the assets they manage, remain custodied at their firm. Yet many times it happens that managers who promised or led an advisor to believe they would be the natural successor to an older advisor's relationships then turn around, recant, and offer the relationships to someone else that might serve the manager's needs at that given moment in time.

With these scenarios, it would be helpful to an investor simply to ask the financial advisor if he has any expectations of following or merging with another advisor's book of business. Similarly, an investor should ask if an advisor had any relationship competition with other advisors within the firm. Many more reasons exist that could cause an advisor to jump ship and find greener or gentler pastures. But for the moment, the aforementioned causes are a good starting place for a client to inquire about an advisor's internal firm relationships. The less difficulty an advisor has within the structure of his firm leads to a better situation for the advisor and, subsequently, a potentially calmer and beneficial relationship for the client.

Revolving Advisors

One significant yet unspoken practice within large brokerage firms involves a firm's habitual pattern of churning in and out young new financial advisors through their training programs. As the basic entry point to the wealth management profession, most starry-eyed young advisors have no choice but to obtain their initial licensing and establishment in the profession through large wire houses, banks, or big-name brokerage firms. In order to proceed with the training and licensure, many trainee advisors are essentially forced to sell their soul and first unborn child to the devil just for the privilege of being able to affiliate with the wire house. In other words, the contract agreements firms oftentimes impose upon new financial advisor trainees make it prohibitively expensive or acutely restrictive for a new trainee advisor to build and maintain a successful practice that can grow through the years.

Making the cut

Rough numbers estimate that about 95 percent of people who attempt to enter the profession and successfully get licensed no longer practice as financial advisors within five years of their initial licensure. This is due to many reasons. First, the fact of the matter is that there are only so many high-net-worth client prospects in the nation.

The majority of the highest account value clients are already spoken for among wealth management professionals who have been in the industry for decades. This leaves a rookie advisor the smaller retail clients to choose from. In order to meet production demands from the wire houses, a new advisor would either have to be lucky enough to already have relationships with investors of large account size or else the advisor would have to glean enough smaller account clients to piece together a sustainable book of business.

Allegorically speaking, many large firms could be compared to Pharaoh Ramses in the story of Moses. When the Hebrew asked how they could make bricks without hay, the pharaoh demanded that they would have to glean the fields by night to effectively scrape enough material together to meet production. In a similar manner, many new trainee advisors are left with no choice but to glean smaller groupings of accounts just to make ends meet. The sad truth is that so many rookie advisors are not successful in gleaning enough critical mass together to create a sustainable book of business. Therefore, the new advisor will often burn out or else be let go by their affiliative firm.

Advisor-firm stipulated agreements

Naturally, wealth management firms, wire houses, and banks operate to make money, build new relationships, and grow the total assets managed by the firm. This is all well and good as part of free enterprise. The problem comes in when those firms use new incoming trainees as a means to acquire new relationships with no intention of retaining the new advisor. What most large firms who train new advisors recognize is that it is still cost effective to train new advisors, onboard those advisors' personal relationships as clients, and then terminate those new advisors if they cannot meet the firm's continually increasing quarterly or annual production demands.

The trick used by firms here is the stipulation in trainee agreements that all new client relationships belong to the firm and not the financial advisor. Should the new financial advisor leave the firm or be let go by the firm, then the advisor has lost control of the relationships due to the trainee contract. As firms cycle in new trainee advisors on a yearly basis or other time frame, the firms retain the new clients' assets gathered by the new advisors and then show the advisors the door once they have served their maximum use for the firm's objectives. Fortunately, I never experienced this scenario in my career. But unfortunately for many wealth management profession hopefuls, this is the sad status of the revolving door at large firms and wire houses.

As a retail investor or new client, it is imperative that you understand the relationship your prospective advisor has with the firm. If you select to entrust your funds and accounts with a large brokerage firm or wire house, it may be prudent to select an advisor who has over ten years of continued experience at that same firm. With such a time frame, odds could be slightly better that your advisor will continue to manage your accounts with that same firm for quite some time without interruption or transition to a new broker dealer.

At a large firm, if you select an advisor who is relatively new to the business or young, it could be prudent to ensure that the young advisor is already part of a team with an older advisor so a succession may already be in place or a sustainable book of business may already be built. Many new advisors who work solo sadly get tossed to the wind and shown the door by management, leaving the advisor with no foreseeable path forward. Working with an independent advisor, you are less likely to encounter these structural industry problems. The independent advisor will be less likely to have unattainable goals imposed upon him my management and will likely have much more control over his practice.

At any rate, it is important to understand that large firms often do not treat their youngling advisors well. Rather, they often use them solely as a means to bring in new assets. The firm may then separate or terminate the newly trained advisor. This kind of change can be detrimental to an investor. Forced advisor swaps caused by upper management machinations can cause an investor to lose years of steady, continuous relationship growth. If a client-advisor relationship is abruptly ended midstream by a firm, any developed relationship and understanding may suffer. Compounded account growth could also be harmed. And last, a client loses precious time in this scenario by having to develop a new relationship with a new advisor.

Advisor Longevity: Prudent Lengths of Time when Selecting an Advisor

Choosing a financial professional to work with also requires an investigation into the tenure of that professional with a specific firm or how long the professional has been licensed. As a general rule of thumb, most financial advisors who have been in the business under five years are still coalescing and developing their convictions around various strategies to manage accounts. Many younger advisors will rely on third-party money managers to manage the actual funds in an account while they continue to grow their book of business.

As the years pass and as a financial advisor has had opportunities to endure successive market corrections or crashes, the advisor should become more adept at recognizing market patterns and cycles. Yet in the early years of a financial advisor's career, if he or she hasn't already spent a decade or more outside of the profession studying market trends, a financial advisor may not be versed enough in knowing how to respond to market volatility to protect your accounts. So here are some rules of thumb to think about when investigating an advisor's length of time in the profession or with a firm.

Ideally, a client would be able to find a financial advisor who has remained with the same firm for several decades. Unfortunately, this is not common to find. Unlike a few generations ago when a person could spend an entire career with the same company or firm, the nature of today's society makes it untenable to remain in the same place. With the fast pace of change throughout many industries, most workers find themselves navigating new relationships or affiliations every several years. The wealth management industry is no exception to this fact of an ever-changing working environment.

Affiliation rotation

A reasonable expectation would be for a financial advisor to work with anywhere between three and six wealth management firms over a twenty- or thirty-year career if that advisor chooses to remain in the role of financial advisor without moving up to a management position or start his own independent RIA in the future. With this expectation, it wouldn't be uncommon to need to follow your advisor through several firm transitions should you choose to maintain relationship continuity with an advisor you like.

The transition process can be relatively easy for most clients. The advisor will have done all the necessary legwork of paperwork and product investigation to serve the client in the same manner they had always been doing. If a financial advisor is a principal of his own RIA, then there should be no major custodian affiliation changes over a long period of time since the principal controls many aspects of a firm's operations. Only rarely will an RIA firm principal make major changes to the structure of his firm.

The thing that a client should be vigilant with is excessive advisor transitions among firms. An investor can easily find an advisor's firm affiliation history through a quick read of his FINRA BrokerCheck record or SEC record. When an investor sees that an advisor has jumped ship many times, say three or more times within a five-year period, then an investor should be wary of such an advisor since the advisor may be unstable or unable to create a solid book of business that can continue into the foreseeable future. How stable would you feel as a client if your advisor needed to move to different pastures that often? Stability is a longed-for ideal in the wealth management and financial advisory field. Yet at times, especially during volatile markets, finding that stability in an advisor can sometimes feel like searching for the Holy Grail. Length of tenure with a firm can often be a sign of stability within a financial advisor that can help reduce your stress as client.

One last comment about advisor tenure relates to transitions during major market upheavals. It seems every seven to ten year at a minimum, the economy endures a major disruption caused either by war, industry collapse, natural disasters, or some other unforeseen event. When these major disruptions occur, many advisors are often forced to transition from their current affiliated firm to another. More often than not, these transitions are due to the ever-changing demands of a wire house's management that creates an unstable situation for the advisor. Rather than focusing on continuity of their advisors' practices, many large firms will instead turn their focus to the possibility of squeezing every dime out of a bad situation, so to speak.

The takeaway from this scenario is that it is relatively common for financial advisors to make one of their career transitions during major economic crises or upheavals, such as the tech bubble bursting in the early 2000s, the financial crisis of 2008, or even now during the COVID-19 pandemic crisis at the time of the writing of this book. It should not come as any worrisome indicator that an advisor makes a major move during a financial crisis or during a recession. On the contrary, it is rather common, and many advisors do just that. While there exist many reasons for a financial advisor to change firms or affiliations, monitoring the stability of length of time with a firm or between firms is just as important as understanding why the advisor made the transition.

Broker Protocol: Friend to the Firm, Foe to the Advisor and Investor

The last topic we will discuss related to your financial advisor's relationship with his firm is a regulatory concept known as the broker protocol. In the most basic terms, this protocol agreement dictates how and who a financial advisor may communicate with, solicit from, or continue to do business with when the financial advisor decides to change affiliations with broker dealers or major wire houses. Due to the frequent movement and relocation of financial advisors among firms, many of the largest wire houses and banks that provide wealth management services decided to come to an agreement, known as the broker protocol, which allows financial advisors to switch to other firms without fear of retaliation, clawbacks, or litigation from their former firm.

Clean breaks? Not always.

However, the stipulations in this agreement can be very restrictive. For instance, the protocol agreement can define which clients a financial advisor is allowed to take with them when they leave a firm. The agreement can also be so controlling to the point where a financial advisor is no longer allowed to reach out to their former clients under pain of financial restitution due to the advisor's former firm. Essentially, these kind of protocol agreements place golden handcuffs upon advisors.

Most large firms decided to become party to this broker protocol agreement around 2004 and have remained enjoined to it ever since. Yet reassessments by some large firms led them to leave the protocol agreement. So what impact does this have to you as an individual investor? By leaving the broker protocol, a firm is making a statement that the firm, and not the individual financial advisor, owns the relationship with the client. In essence, if your financial advisor is not protected under some broker protocol arrangement, then the advisor will lose clients, and potentially much of his book of business, if he decides to move to another firm.

Who controls the relationship? Firm, advisor, or client?

There is much argument as to whether it is ethical or moral for a brokerage firm to say they 100 percent own the relationship to a client and essentially own those clients' accounts as opposed to the financial advisor. After all, if the financial advisor is the one who found, developed, and maintained the relationship with the client, shouldn't the financial advisor be able to maintain that relationship for his efforts and to be able to serve clients with continuity and without fear of retaliation from a prior firm?

For my own practice's purposes, I have chosen to affiliate with custodians and broker dealers who recognize and respect my right as a financial advisor to independently maintain relationships with my clients no matter which firm I choose to affiliate with. In my opinion, that seems to be the most moral, fair, and respectful decision a firm principal or broker dealer can offer to me and my clients. In contrast, those firms who insist through contracts that advisors who work within their firm have no right to maintain their client relationships after they leave are, in my opinion, behaving like greedy squirrels obsessively trying to gather and hoard nuts for the coming winter only for themselves to the detriment of others.

As an investor, it is important to ask the branch manager or upper management of a firm if the advisor you may be working with is subject to the broker protocol or what would happen to the advisor's clients if the advisor chose to switch firms. Of course, a firm cannot stop a client from contacting a former financial advisor they like to business with in an unsolicited manner where the client initiates contact once the advisor has moved to another firm. Just be aware that the advisor may not be able to reach out to you directly if a transition to another firm occurs due to the golden handcuffs that might have been placed on him by his prior firm.

Changes will occur to almost every advisor over the course of their career as an advisor moves from one firm to another or starts their own independent RIA practice. Nothing should worry or stop a client from moving along with an advisor through the years as the advisor grows his business. The key takeaways are to remember to watch out for frequent and a large number of transitions in a short amount of time in addition to the length of time an advisor has remained with their current firm. Whether a firm churns new advisors in and out the door to acquire more assets under management for the firm can also indicate behavioral problems with that firm that could hinder an investors experience while investing.

Last, it is important to question a firm's management, not necessarily the financial advisor, if the broker protocol will apply to the financial advisor. Sometimes even unethical managers won't be upfront or honest about the broker protocol when recruiting new advisors to their firms. In the end, a financial advisor may have been misled by a brokerage firm into believing the advisor could retain relationships to clients only to have the firm pull a sleight of hand and recant that understanding. This situation ultimately can lead to litigation between the financial advisor and firm, leaving the client less well served.

CHAPTER 3

Moral Obligation to Moral Hazard
Conflicts in the Wealth Accumulation Process

One of the most relevant stories relating to money and wealth in the Bible speaks of Matthew the tax collector and his conversion from viewing money as a means to an end to one of serving others. Too often, many financial practitioners lose focus that their main purpose through their careers is to help others secure a solid foundation for their financial futures. Instead, many financial professionals merely use their occupation to enrich themselves at the expense of their clients, without regard to how they should be serving those clients.

As we begin this chapter touching on moral obligation and moral hazard, we will define and learn about the differences between types of accounts (discretionary versus nondiscretionary) as well as the obligations required of a financial advisor to their clients (fiduciary versus nonfiduciary). Looking at these terms, a clearer picture may come into focus to help you decide which kind of investment account you may want to establish in addition to which type of financial professional serves your needs. The variations in these account and financial professional types may mean the difference between having conflicts arise with your financial professional or having no conflicts arise.

Discretionary

The first concept we will discuss is one regarding the amount of discretion or control that your financial advisor will be allowed to have over your accounts. Many different types of account structures exist across the spectrum of the investing world, and they even often vary among brokerage firms. Yet the one difference to understand is how much control you will be giving to your financial advisor in order to manage your funds and accounts.

For the purposes of financial discussion, the term *discretionary* essentially means in simple terms that your financial advisor is permitted to choose the selection of investments, amounts to invest in each investment, and the time to invest. If you permit your advisor, through the account agreements, to serve in a discretionary capacity, then you are, for the most part, giving your advisor free will to act in the manner he sees fit at any given time. There are some pros and cons to choosing this type of account.

Trading approvals

On the plus side, allowing your advisor to serve in a discretionary fashion can often be much more efficient and time saving than a nondiscretionary account. For a discretionary account, your financial advisor does not need to get verbal or written approval every time the advisor recommends making a trade or investment for your account. When the advisor is free to make investment choices for an account as he sees fit, it creates a much more efficient scenario where the advisor can spend more time researching and looking for suitable investments for your accounts as opposed to frequently and repetitively obtaining your approval for every single investment as it is placed in the account.

On the other hand, a discretionary account can be problematic if the advisor you choose to work with does not consistently apply the investment objectives and risk tolerance that you indicated to the advisor when the relationship was first established. When an investor becomes a new client of a financial advisor, the advisor has an obligation to ask, understand, and receive documented verification of exactly how much risk a client is willing to tolerate while investing and how investment time frames come into play for an investor. Sometimes, over the course of a relationship, an advisor may lose sight of the original tolerable risk levels approved by a client. The advisor may then decide to take risks in investments that go beyond what the client understood to be acceptable. This is where a significant moral hazard comes into play.

Excessive risk

When excessive risks in discretionary accounts are taken beyond a client's original intent and understanding, the end result for a client's investments and portfolio could result in losses or the dissolution of a successful relationship with that advisor. When allowing an advisor to use discretionary authority over an account, it is imperative for a client to get a clear understanding of the advisor's exact timing and methodology for timing purchases and sales of investments in an account in addition to which types of funds or products will precisely be used. The risk levels of those products and potential timing of investments are two of the greatest factors that will determine whether your portfolio will grow through the years.

One last item to discuss relevant to discretionary account types is the fact that not all brokerage firms or wire houses allow their advisors to use discretionary account with their clients. Due to the legal liabilities for financial advisors and wealth management firms, many companies and advisors will not agree to serve clients using discretionary accounts. Later in this book, we will discuss litigation and risks for advisors to their practices due to the regulatory nature of the wealth management field. But what is important to know here is that many financial advisors and brokerage firms become subjected to fraudulent claims by unethical attorneys or greedy clients who have figured out how to game the legal system where financial services are involved.

These attempts and false claims against financial advisors have become commonplace on a monthly and yearly basis that many attorneys have formed entire practices and business models on such extortionist behavior. Most of the time the fraudulent claims are thrown out or successfully defended against by financial advisors and firms. However, the ever-present threat of claims against advisors makes the use of discretionary accounts problematic and, many times, costly for the firm or advisor. Hence, many firms and advisors will simply refuse to take on discretionary accounts as part of their practice.

Nondiscretionary

The flip side to the discretionary account is the nondiscretionary account. Under this type of account, an advisor does not have the authority, per the account agreements, to select and place investments at will as the advisor sees fit. Instead, the advisor must, under this account structure, obtain verbal communication or written approval every single time a trade is placed in an account. As one can imagine, this can be a very time-consuming and inconvenient method to manage portfolios if the financial advisor uses frequent portfolio rebalancing and trading to achieve investment goals.

Client makes the call

Nondiscretionary accounts tend to account for the majority of account types across firms and across the wealth management profession. With this type of account structure, a firm or financial advisor reduces their liability to potential claims brought against them by a client. The interpretation for nondiscretionary accounts is that the investment selections and timing of investments in an account are governed by the client's actual directives and approvals as opposed to the financial advisor's own decisions. When the client is making the actual decision for the investments in their account, the regulatory viewpoint is then that the client is responsible for the performance or losses of the account and not necessarily the financial advisor. With this interpretation compared to discretionary accounts, it is very easy to see why financial advisors and firms would prefer to use only nondiscretionary accounts to protect themselves from liability.

One of the positives to using nondiscretionary accounts is that the frequency of trading in your accounts may be significantly reduced. This could lead to a more passive strategy of investing, which will be explained later in this book, that allows the account to grow without major or significant changes to the individual account holdings. If an advisor is not allowed to trade frequently within an account, either through the use of discretionary accounts or frequent verified approval by the client in nondiscretionary accounts, then there is lowered chance the accounts may be churned by an advisor to meet production goals. What is of vital importance to a new client is to understand that if a financial advisor places trades in a nondiscretionary account without a client's express approval, then the advisor is committing a breach of contract that breaks several regulations. It is important for a client to beware of any activity in a nondiscretionary account that is not expressly approved by the client.

One last explanation to discuss is precisely how a financial advisor may obtain the necessary approvals to trade for a client in a nondiscretionary account. If an account is structured as a nondiscretionary account, then a financial advisor must follow strict protocols to obtain a client's approval to invest in a product at a given time. Usually, most firms accept verbal approval via a phone call between a financial advisor and their client to obtain the required approval. E-mails and communications over social media are not allowed by regulation as acceptable methods to gain a client's approval to trade within an account. Signed and dated written letters also sometimes apply to the types of products that a client is willing to permit an advisor to trade.

Additional directives

As a note to this, many times, clients can write specific directives as to what specific types of products or in which allocation concentrations may be applied to a client's accounts. These specific directives can be used on either discretionary or nondiscretionary accounts. Whether you choose, or are permitted by an investment firm, using discretionary or nondiscretionary accounts can have impact on the ease with which you relate to your financial advisor. Bear in mind, your financial advisor will usually have a specific manner in which he is accustomed to working with regard to discretionary or nondiscretionary accounts. It is up to you, as a client, to decide at the beginning of the relationship with a new advisor just how much freedom you want to allow that advisor to use when helping to manage your portfolio for long-term growth.

Fiduciary

With an understanding of the difference between discretionary and nondiscretionary account types, it is also important to have a solid understanding of the thirty-thousand-foot view of the concept of a financial advisor's fiduciary obligation to a client. The concept of the fiduciary versus the nonfiduciary role an advisor has toward a client acutely impacts the duties the advisor owes to the client. The term *fiduciary* is casually thrown about in advertisements and commercials by many investment firms. In fact, it has sort of become a catch-all phrase often overused by firms who want to present an image of responsible stewardship over investors' money and accounts.

Serving the faithful

To put it in allegorical terms, the Gospel's tale of Matthew's conversion after serving as a tax collector for the Roman Empire showed that he finally decided to put the best interests of his spiritual kinsmen above those of the empire. Initially, his life took a path to serve a corrupt imperial entity for the primary purpose of protecting himself. When the time came for Jesus to show him another way of living, Matthew chose to discard his prioritization of self-interest. Matthew then began to focus on how he could properly serve others. Similarly, when dealing with fiduciary duty, by definition, the financial advisor is required to put the interests of clients first before the advisor's own interests. There are many ways potential conflicts could arise and moral obligation can be pushed aside. As we delve into the term *fiduciary*, here are some general concepts to understand.

Fiduciaries serve in a role of trust to the people they serve. In the context of financial services and wealth management, this basically means that a financial advisor is required to put the best interests of the client first. This can take many forms. For instance, one example of an advisor adequately performing his fiduciary duty would be for the advisor to offer a client an array of products with different costs. If the advisor chooses or recommends to the client a product that may be less expensive but less profitable to the advisor's fees or commissions, then the advisor is most likely putting the interests of the client's account first before his own profit. By taking on the role of fiduciary, the financial advisor is legally responsible for the management of a client's money, much in the same way that an executor would be responsible for someone's estate after their passing or a power of attorney may be given to someone over another person's well-being.

Finding a fiduciary advisor

How can a new investor or client know if a financial professional is a fiduciary? Well, one key concept to understand in the wealth management field is that advisors who structure their practice by charging an annual fee are typically fiduciaries. By regulatory definition under the purview of the SEC, fee-based financial advisors typically have different registrations than broker dealers. Fee-based advisors are usually either an RIA, as discussed prior, or else they work within an RIA firm's framework as an investment advisor representative.

The name terminology of financial professional types can often overlap or become confusing to the general Main Street investor. But it is critically important to understand the precise title and structure of a financial advisor's practice to know if he serves in a fiduciary capacity. One way to know if a financial advisor serves in a fiduciary capacity is to ask if he has passed the Series 66 test. Another way to find a fiduciary status is to search for the advisor's record on the SEC's Investment Advisor Registration Depository. If you find the advisor on the SEC's IARD and his status is active and in good standing, odds are you are dealing with a professional who is a fiduciary.

From the perspective of the client, it would be more advantageous to work with a financial advisor who is a fiduciary. In doing so, you'll have knowledge that your financial professional is held to a higher standard than many other professionals in the field. Also, it is an indication that the advisor passed through a more rigorous academic and training standard than one who has not. And last, working with a fiduciary can offer some additional peace of mind in knowing that your financial advisor could less likely be prone to conflicts of interest when managing your assets.

Nonfiduciary

Compared to fiduciaries, nonfiduciaries are held to a lesser standard when serving their clients. Nonfiduciary financial advisors are held to what is called a suitability standard. One could go into extreme detail explaining the difference between the fiduciary standard versus the suitability standard. In fact, over the past decade, it has become a rather contentious debate topic within legal and financial professional circles, leading all the way up to arguments between successive presidential administrations. Essentially, the argument comes down to which categories and groupings of financial professionals would be held to the fiduciary standard versus the suitability standard. What is important to know is that selecting a financial advisor who is only held to the suitability standard may not serve your financial plan as attentively as one who holds themselves to a fiduciary standard via regulatory testing.

The lesser standard

Nonfiduciaries typically hold a lower level of testing achievement and may not have all the licensing that a fiduciary may have. For instance, one way to know if a financial advisor is only a nonfiduciary is to see if he only has a Series 6 or Series 7 testing credential. Nonfiduciaries are commonly called broker dealers within the industry, whereas fiduciaries are commonly called investment advisor representatives or RIAs. Nonfiduciaries typically receive their compensation only via commission per transaction or trade.

Unlike fiduciaries, they are not permitted under current regulations to charge a percentage-based fee off the total of your account's assets held with the advisor's firm. This is a brief explanation of how advisor compensation differentiates fiduciaries from nonfiduciaries. However, how does the reduced level of standard of care impact you as an investor and your accounts? Let's take a quick look into this aspect of the fiduciary versus suitability standard.

Suitability versus fiduciary

If your financial advisor is a nonfiduciary, then he is only legally required to provide you services under the suitability standard. In other words, since he is not a fiduciary, he does not necessarily have to put the client's interests first. It can easily be guessed how this could open up the client-advisor relationship to conflicts of interest and disagreements. Under suitability, your financial advisor as broker only has to have a reasonable basis that recommended securities for a client are suitable based upon the customers stated age, other investments, tax status, financial needs, investment experience, and a few other criteria that can be found through FINRA's website. As a nonfiduciary, these requirements alone do not address the issue of trust and responsibility an advisor would have to deliver to a client as a fiduciary.

Regulatory roulette

If you are a bit confused as to the difference between the fiduciary standard and the suitability standard, take comfort in knowing that you are not alone. The minutiae and hairsplitting differences between the two standards even confound many industry professionals and lawyers as changes to regulations became more muddled over the past several years. Entire debates ensued among the Department of Labor, FINRA, the SEC, and the most recent presidential administrations over how many advisors would be required to be held to the fiduciary standard as opposed to the suitability standard. While the Department of Labor pushed to expand fiduciary requirements for more brokers based on licensure during the Obama administration, the same Department of Labor rescinded those additional requirements several years later. The regulatory teeter-totter caused an immense amount of stress and confusion within the wealth management industry.

As for myself and my own practice, I immediately became licensed and registered as a fiduciary upon entering the profession and currently operate as an accredited investment fiduciary. In my view, I have always held that conviction that interests of the client should come first before any other considerations, just as Matthew turned his efforts to eventually serving others in the Gospel. As a new investor or client, you should ask yourself whether you want the role of your advisor to be one of trust and responsibility for your portfolio (as a fiduciary) or if you simply want your advisor to serve as a transactional broker (a nonfiduciary), who is essentially only there to process transactions and offer limited advice for you.

Your selection of one versus the other will have an impact on the total cost you pay to your financial advisor over the course of a year as well as the expected level of personal attention and service you receive. If I were not practicing as a professional within the wealth management industry and if I were looking to hire an advisor, personally, I would want to ensure that the advisor would be held to the higher fiduciary standard. However, every investor has different objectives and different expectations of how much they want their advisor to be involved in their comprehensive life. Therefore, the industry presents these two overarching yet different financial advisor types regarding standard of care to the general investing public.

CHAPTER 4

Who Is in the Details—God or the Devil?
Techniques for Consideration

Some say that God is in the details. Others say that the devil is in the details. Regardless of which camp of thought you find yourself in, it would be appropriate to say that digging into the details of any investment strategy or portfolio plan is of vital importance. Perhaps you are the kind of person who despised math, calculus, statistics, and economics in school. Or perhaps those skills are second nature to you and you enjoy poring over endless charts and computations. Either way, having a sound understanding of the potential strategies your financial advisor can offer you will help you determine the long-term behavior of your portfolio.

In this chapter, we will investigate some technical considerations and the actual mechanics of how financial advisors implement their strategies either on your behalf or with your personal input. Regarding investment strategies, there exist two major groups of thought. One believes that taking an active approach to trading and managing money by using rotation of positions in an account is the more beneficial way to go for long-term growth. The other school of thought believes that establishing a solid set of positions within an account and holding those positions as is for a very long period of time with little change is the more efficient approach to reach long-term growth.

Separate from these two approaches, differences also exist among financial advisors as to whether technical factors of the market should be paid close attention to or if the more abstract psychological trends of market behavior should govern account management strategies. And last, the approach that each individual financial advisor takes toward the selection of investment products rounds out the major topics to consider when taking a closer look into the mechanics of investing. While each of the aforementioned items factor into a well-rounded portfolio plan or investment strategy, not every advisor gives each of them equal weight. Upfront, it is good to go into your interviews of prospective financial advisors for you equipped with a basic knowledge of these concepts and various strategies. Doing so will help you to know which direction your portfolio could be headed and also help you to avoid some traps that each of these approaches may present as you work to build your financial foundation for retirement.

Active versus Passive Management: The Endless Battle

The never-ending argument that seems to continue decade after decade within the wealth management profession revolves around whether positions within an account should be frequently traded or rather held for a long period of time to achieve consistent growth. Wealth managers who use a frequent trading and allocation rotation strategy are known to be using active or tactical management. In contrast, wealth managers who prefer to leave positions unchanged within an account for long periods of time, such as in years, are known to be using passive or strategic management.

Year after year and decade after decade, debates ensue among financial professionals about which method is better. Each camp of thought argues that their method is better to be used at certain times in economic market cycles. In reality, both sides of the argument attempt to prove to clients how the other side's methods will underperform over different time frames in order to sway opinion and gather new assets.

Which one to choose

To be frank, I have always held the position that both strategies can be useful. The critical factor for an advisor is to know specifically at which points in a market cycle we currently are and then apply one strategy versus the other. Therefore, I have always tried to remain impartial and agnostic toward both methods regarding their merits. However, for my own professional practice, I will openly admit that I have always preferred the active or tactical management and tend to use that method with greater continuity. This is for several reasons.

For one thing, I have seen too many times over the multiple corrections and market crashes of the past thirty years when investors' accounts take a severe hit and are not able to recover in sufficient time for retirement using the passive or strategic method. Active or tactical management tends to be nimbler in reacting to constant market changes throughout the years. Furthermore, it is my opinion that holding positions locked in a passive or strategic method does not provide enough cash flow flexibility when an investor needs it. Life always throws curveballs and most of us cannot predict when they will be thrown our way. Therefore, wouldn't it be better to know you have the flexibility to use your hard-earned money when you need to if monetary emergencies arise through the years of your investing timeline? Here, we'll begin to take a closer look into the details of both of these strategies.

Passive management

First let's take a look at what asset allocation is and how passive or strategic methods are applied to allocation. As a client, you should ask and be very clear with your financial advisor about which approach the advisor plans to use to grow your portfolio over time. It is well established that more than 90 percent of portfolio volatility can be attributed to how assets are allocated or how an investor chooses to allocate investments among a variety of different asset classes. For example, an investor may adjust the amount of his or her portfolio to allocate to growth or value stocks in large-, mid-, and small-cap companies—as well as to corporate, municipal, and government bonds and cash—based on his or her individual goals, risk tolerance, and time horizon.

The allocation decision is frequently backward-looking, based on past performance of the asset classes. This approach is classified as strategic asset management. Strategic asset management responds to market forces after the fact. Traditionally, strategic asset management means to buy and hold, and then periodically rebalance the portfolio, selling investments in higher performing asset classes and purchasing investments in lower performing asset classes, to bring the portfolio back to its original asset allocation.

Portfolio management could also take an integrated approach where a financial advisor uses both strategic and tactical methods simultaneously or perhaps separate the two strategies among different accounts for a client. The important distinctions between strategic asset management and tactical asset management mean that many investors are interested in using tactical asset management strategies to support their strategic asset management goals. Your financial advisor has a variety of resources and a robust set of tools to incorporate tactical asset management strategies into a holistic plan to help build and preserve your wealth. So if passive or strategic asset management is a backward-looking or after-the-fact approach toward market behavior, let's then take a look at how active or tactical management works.

Active management

To put in plainest terms, active or tactical asset management anticipates market forces now and for the future. Tactical asset management is a more dynamic, forward-looking form of asset allocation that seeks to adjust asset allocations to expose investors to capital building and to capital preservation opportunities based on macroeconomic and leading indicators for various markets, sectors, and asset classes. The effects of globalization, market volatility, and rapid economic changes over recent years have created renewed interest in this form of asset allocation.

There are some benefits of tactical asset management over strategic management. Employing some degree of tactical asset management may offer the chance to benefit from—and manage risks from—ever-changing opportunities and threats. For example, a strategic asset allocation of 60 percent equities may be maintained. However, in a tactical move, the ratio of domestic to foreign stock within that 60 percent equities position may be reallocated based on indicators, measures, and the chosen tactical methodology. And instead of selling winners to purchase losers through traditional rebalancing, it may help improve overall portfolio performance.

The mechanical details

How does tactical asset management actually work? Generally speaking, tactical asset management strategies attempt to maximize risk-adjusted returns by identifying and taking advantage of relative mispricing across asset classes. To accomplish this, tactical asset allocation uses a variety of measures to evaluate current market status and forecast potential future opportunities and risks. These measures include technical, fundamental, and quantitative indicators. Based on these indicators, buy-or-sell decisions are made based on tested, disciplined, and systematic methodologies. And as brief introduction for the novice investor, we will quickly look at a few different types of indicators to help give you some rudimentary understanding of the concepts before going to your financial advisor to discuss investment strategy.

The first type of indicator is known as a technical indicator. Price and volume trends over time may help establish floor and ceiling values for securities to help inform buy-and-sell decisions. These patterns may also provide advanced signals to shift allocation weights from equities to treasuries, or vice versa. For example, a head and shoulders pattern in an equity market chart may suggest an opportune time to switch from stocks to T-bills. The next type of indicator is the fundamental indicator. Financial and economic indicators that reflect overall market valuation may help investors choose which sectors or asset classes are more opportune than others. For example, one such measure compares stock dividend yields with bond interest. Stocks are said to be expensive when the market's dividend yield is low relative to that of ten-year notes. And a third type of indicator are quantitative measures.

Applying quantitative market measures or variables to predictive models may help identify appropriate trades. For example, a model may be designed to identify potential market pullbacks based on the interplay of stock price movements with the money supply, dividend yields, and economic activity. These types of indicators dive into very technical matters of the financial field. Unless you want to take the time to do intense academic research into each of these technical factors for your own personal interest as an investor, my suggestion would be to leave the application of these technical indicators to your financial advisor. Yet I would emphasize that, at a bare minimum, you should be informed by your advisor which of these methods and indicators he predominantly uses in his practice.

Strategy interference and surprises

As can be seen from this discussion of active versus passive management and some of the detailed factors that go into their application, it can become rather complicated. That it is why it is best to leave the technical application to your financial advisor. Many times, I have seen clients interfere with a defined strategy that their financial advisor lays out when the client interjects their own demands for buying certain securities or making withdrawals from an account contrary to the original objectives that were established by the client and advisor early on in the relationship. Consistency on the part of the client is of paramount importance in the client-advisor relationship. It is the duty of the client to clearly state objectives at the beginning of a relationship with a financial advisor so the advisor knows precisely how he needs to apply methodologies to fit your unique financial goals and retirement planning.

Additionally, should any significant changes occur in your life, such as a job change, marriage, child birth, or divorce, it is absolutely imperative that you notify your financial advisor immediately.

A financial advisor needs adequate lead time to adjust a portfolio to keep it on track when major changes occur in your life. As a general rule of thumb, you, as a client, should proactively reach out to your financial advisor at least once a year to inform him of any changes over the past year or any anticipated changes in the coming year. I cannot count how many times clients either withheld information from me or waited too long to tell me. The subsequent result was an unnecessary shuffling of strategies, accounts, or positions that could have been avoided had the client been up front. Quick communication on the client's part can save a lot of trouble down the road.

While clients remain responsible to keep their advisor informed at all times, it is equally as critical for your financial advisor to inform you of anticipated time frames to reach your goals and succeed in your retirement planning. One trap that often occurs in the client-advisor relationship involves misunderstanding applicable time frames to succeed using different strategies. For instance, some strategies' success may depend on whether the asset management strategy is based upon long-term growth. On the other hand, the success may be based on short-term trading or market timing.

Active versus passive management differentiation depends upon whether trading is based on timing opportunity in the market versus waiting to see held securities' reactions over time. The pitfall to the investor's trap here is failing to understand the frequency and justification of your advisor's recommendation or trading pattern. Details not fully explained or misunderstood by the investor count for many failed attempts to grow portfolio assets. As a client, be sure to ask and understand these aforementioned details.

Technocrat or Psychologist: Harnessing both for Prudent Investing

Now that we've taken a look into the technical details of different methods to apply investment management, let's take a look into some other details pertaining to how your financial advisor views the overall markets. Another dividing factor that causes different approaches to the markets involves whether your advisor prefers to view market behavior through a technical lens or a more psychological lens. The investment markets, as confounding as they are, can be broken down into two main patterns, which are technical analysis and behavioral analysis. Granted, trying to generalize the complexity of the entire investment markets into these two categories is an extreme oversimplification to say the least. But for our purposes in *Traps of Treasure*, these two categories are very good springboards to jump into the most basic understanding of market behavior and analysis.

The technocrat

The first understanding of the markets takes a very quantitative look at investments. A financial advisor who spends much time analyzing charts and quantitative spreadsheets is often called a technician or a chartist. For this book, we will use the broad term *technocrat* to group any financial advisor or analyst who operates in this manner. As for myself, I have practiced my entire financial career predominantly using the chartist application toward the markets. Chartists will spend hours poring over detailed data to attempt to foresee coming patterns for individual securities or the major market indexes. They will compile historical data charts over multiple time frames in an attempt to see patterns in trend lines through the years and decades.

Sometimes, in the markets, history can have a tendency to repeat itself, although this is not always the case. By searching for patterns in the charts of positions over time, chartists attempt to look for good opportunities to buy positions at historically low prices. Equally as important, chartists attempt to see in charts and numerical data when securities become overpriced relative to their historical earnings or other metrics. Using a technocrat's methods can often successfully be applied to harvest gains and protect from losses during market corrections. If a technocrat is adept enough at their application toward account trading and management, then the client's account should be able to benefit from both the upswings and downswings in the market, when combined at different stages of the market cycles.

The psychologist

The other understanding of the markets takes a more psychological look at how the markets tend to move in unison or diverge. Here in *Traps of Treasure*, we will use the word *psychologist* to describe financial advisors who lean more toward researching the behavioral trends of the markets. To explain, much of the growth or downfall of specific investment securities and the market indexes can be attributed to how many investors across all categories attempt to invest in the same security or in the same way. When too many people try to buy the same type of security, a situation can occur where that trade becomes what is termed crowded. In other words, the trading price of the security in relation to its actual value based on the company's underlying fundamental data becomes excessively high. This presents a dangerous scenario for retail investors if they or their financial advisors are not able to recognize these inflated prices. If they don't, the security becomes at risk of quick devaluation where investors could lose a lot of money quickly.

The most obvious example of this scenario occurred between 2000 and 2002 during the tech bubble burst indicated during the severe drop in the NASDAQ Composite Index. Euphoria took over the masses, and too many people decided to buy into technology companies that had no intrinsic value. The end result was a very rude awakening in the early 2000s for many people's retirement portfolios and 401(k). The psychologists of the wealth management world will spend much of their efforts attempting to find situations such as this. Or put in simpler terms, they are keeping an eye out for the herd of buffalo that is about ready to run off a cliff. Like the buffalo, herd mentality can affect retail and institutional investors en masse as well, leading to a significant amount of wealth destruction if not recognized, averted, and protected from.

With the two main categories of financial advisor market mindsets, technocrat and psychologist, you could ask and argue which view better develops a sound retirement plan. My answer is simple. They both are of equal importance. A beginning investor's potential trap is selecting a financial advisor who believes in viewing the market only through one lens. The two market-viewing mindsets intend to be fully complementary to each other. Neither one should take precedence over the other.

Just as much can be learned by researching market behavioral patterns as it can through studying charts and mathematical data. As a new client, verify that your financial advisor understands and implements both of these methodologies to manage your portfolio. Traps lurk around every corner when you and your financial advisor do not recognize euphoric buying quickly in certain securities or market sectors. Additional traps also open in the floor beneath you when neither observes technical trend line risks of those securities or market sectors.

The Investment Product Buffet

As we wrap up this highly technical chapter pertaining to more mechanical aspects of investing, we will finally take a look at what kind of investment products may be available to the retail investing public. *Traps of Treasure* makes no recommendations as to one product type over another and does not address the explanations of the various types of products available. Each type of investment product has its own very specific function, construction, and suitable place and time for its use. What will be said in this book is that it would be prudent, as a new investor or client, to choose a financial professional who structures his practice around highly focalized use of a select few types of investment products.

The specialist or generalist advisor

In other words, it may be prudent for a client to choose an advisor who specializes in only certain segments of the markets as opposed to a generalist who tries to be everything to each of his clients in his book of business. In my experience, generalists do not gather enough understanding of specialized products over time to be able to utilize specialty products in an effective manner. Remember, an infinite number of products exist on the market from which the investor and financial advisor can choose. Rather than try to grasp and implement a large number of those different types, a more effective approach would be to select two or three product types that your financial advisor is most familiar with and allow him to utilize those few product types in a surgical fashion within your portfolio.

As noted on the introduction of this book, many among the masses of retail and general investing public may wonder why they don't succeed as easily or as well as many high-net-worth investors. The average retirement saver usually has an intuitive feeling that the investment world, its platforms, and its products are rigged to benefit only the few at the top of the financial food chain. Well, essentially, that intuitive feeling is correct.

For the most part, there exists a minimum asset cutoff barrier of around half a million dollars of liquid investable assets to separate accredited investors (those considered worth financial institutions' detailed attention) versus the rest of the general public who have under half a million dollars available to invest. What consequence does this class separation have for most of the general investing public? Well, it means that those who do not qualify to be considered accredited investors cannot get access to more complex investments, such as some structured products, third-party money managers with excellent performance, or private equity, to name a few types of investments.

Accredited investing

Of course, there are many more types of investments only reserved for accredited or institutional investors, but we will focus only on what can be made available to the general public. Access to products reserved for high-net-worth investors generally means that they will have a greater chance to compound higher returns over longer periods of time. One way around this imbalance is for a client to ask if their financial advisor can mimic more advanced products through trading in a portfolio in a certain manner. This will be a detailed topic for you and your advisor to discuss. But for the beginner's purposes, it is sufficient to know that it can be done with very attentive detail and precision. You may not be able to mirror the high returns enjoyed by many institutional investors, but you may have a chance to improve your portfolio's returns over time with some added effort by your financial advisor.

In appendix A, I compiled a comprehensive but general list of wealth management products, account types, and types of securities, which, for the most part, the general retail investing public has access to through their financial advisor's platform. Before meeting with a financial advisor, it may be good to familiarize yourself with these terms so you may have a basic knowledge of what he is referring to if you don't have much experience with the investment world. If you are curious about the meaning and definition of these terms, a good resource to use would be *Investopedia*, found on the internet.

Not all these products will be germane to your personal circumstances, but it is a good starting point as you initiate your relationship with a financial professional. Management strategies, market theories, and the endless array of product possibilities present an overwhelming buffet of items to choose from. For the beginning investor, my suggestion would be to allow your financial advisor to guide you in the direction he sees most suitable for your needs. That's what your advisor is there for, namely, to manage the day-to-day operations and framework of your long-term financial plan while you focus on the day-to-day activities of your life, such as your career, family, and friends.

CHAPTER 5

Camels through Needle Eyes
Industry Problems of Self-Interest and Fraud

Have you ever heard the parable of the rich man and the camel trying to pass through a needle's eye? Most of us have. And in that parable, we are told of the requirements for attaining salvation. Not that it was said that it was impossible for a wealthy man to enter into the gates of heaven compared to a camel passing through the eye of a needle. The odds become significantly harder when the pursuit of wealth to the detriment of others is the primary motive for a person's labors. Fraud and self-serving interests of financial professionals manifest themselves in many ways throughout the wealth management profession.

Most of the time, those methods of fraud or sleight of hand are disguised beneath statements of protection for the investor or serving the greater good. And as a new client or beginning investor, it is very hard to decipher the taglines or means by which immoral or unethical financial professionals use false pretenses of serving your needs. Rather, in fact, they are only serving their own interests.

While many of the general public, especially the middle class, wonder precisely how many in the wealth management industry come by their extreme wealth and flaunt an exorbitant lifestyle, the reality is much of it is accumulated through evasive maneuvers by financial professionals. Yet at the same time, fraud and self-interest are not simply a one-way street. Just as there are many financial professionals trying to take advantage of naive or uneducated clients, there exist just as many clients who attempt to game the financial system and immorally bring false claim against financial professionals. The arbitration and litigation arm of the wealth management industry has become a very profitable business model for many attorneys and even the regulatory bodies. Their annual budgets and bottom lines continue to grow as more false claims are brought against many financial professionals or entities when you investigate their successive yearly returns and publicly disclosed financial statements.

There are several ways in which industry self-interest and fraud occur. But herein, we will discuss just a few of the more concerning topics that may affect a new investor relative to their interaction with their financial advisor or the firm that holds their assets. For one thing, many new investors don't always realize exactly how tied a financial advisor's hands are due to constraints or directives of regulatory bodies. Even if a financial advisor wants to do something beneficial for you or something he thinks may be in your best interest as a client, the regulatory bodies, more often than not, will threaten the advisor with fines, suspension, proceedings, and many other strategies to benefit the regulatory agency under the guise of protecting the public's interest.

Another situation that could affect your relationship with your advisor is the ever-present threat of fraudulent claims brought against your advisor by other clients with extortion incentives. Although your financial advisor may have done his job perfectly and with full execution of fiduciary duties to all his clients, it won't stop some investors from trying to financially take advantage of your financial advisor by way of gaming the regulatory bodies and rules. Should these fraudulent attempts against your financial advisor succeed in any way, it could be detrimental to a long-standing and successful relationship you may have had with the professional who serves you. And last, I have often heard over my career from many in the general public who do not have any professional relationship with me that they almost never hear from their financial advisor. Or oftentimes, when they call into their broker, they receive no response back, especially during times of market crisis or volatility. Well, there are reasons for this as well, which we will look at as our last topic of this chapter.

Who's Watching the Watchers?

While many in the media like to take the time to expose fraudulent advisors or the numerous swindlers discovered within the wealth management profession, they rarely investigate unethical or deceptive efforts practiced by the regulators and those who are supposed to govern the wealth management industry as a whole. One way this is brought about is through the lack of attention paid to misleading statements by industry officials. As with many significant overall market appreciations in relatively short time frames throughout the years, underlying risks of painful corrections remain ever present. This remains true even when the media continue to tout stellar performance in multiple sectors and metrics of the domestic economy.

Policy deception

Through the decades, many of the most painful market corrections occurred due to underlying flaws in either the government or private sector policy or outright denial and deception perpetrated by the powers that be or ivory-tower academics. Causes of such market drops were not often fully revealed until after the fact and only after investors lost years of hard-earned gradual growth. The most notable examples in recent history include Black Monday of 1987, the S&L crisis involving the Keating Five of the late '80s to early '90s, the tech bubble burst of the early 2000s, and more recent in the minds of the general public, the housing and derivative instruments collapse that instigated the financial crisis of late 2008. New investors should take it with a grain of salt that the information they are being fed by regulators or those in power may not be accurate or may have another incentive to protect certain groups of people in power.

Some technicians, analysts, and chartists who publicly asserted warnings of such developments before they happened often found themselves ignored or ridiculed by those in the know, only to have their correct assessments completely forgotten after the downfalls occurred. On the other hand, public officials and "economic experts" supposedly well-versed in market behavior made famously incorrect calls that devastated many households and portfolios of the mass investing public. The prime example of this was former Federal Reserve chairman Alan Greenspan's testimony assertions in the mid-2000s that no housing bubble existed. Most adults during that period remember the infamous quotes splashed all over the news in the years subsequent to the housing market's collapse. History proved that statement notoriously incorrect yet with devastating consequences for many Main Street investors but with no accountability placed upon the so-called experts.

Since that notorious wrong call by the former Federal Reserve chair, many officials became tight-lipped or ambiguous when vocalizing opinions. Subsequently, they have swung to the other end of the pendulum to avoid making concrete assertions of any kind. Yet this could also present another extreme that can lead to a market imbalance. It could be said that years of quantitative easing and loose monetary policy created a situation that may unwind unpleasantly for investment portfolios. As well, it could be said that current Federal Reserve policy exhibits flaws that could create the next bubble to burst after so many years of a meandering policy. As an investor, it is important to be aware of the possible forward effect on the economy due to recent years' policy.

Regulatory teeter-totter

When working with a financial professional, vigilance toward the impact that regulators and governing entities have on an advisor's practice cannot be overstated. With the seesaw of regulations going back and forth through the years, it is more likely than not that your advisor will need to modify his business practices or offerings to be nimble enough to respond to the excess burden of compliance. The most recent example of this was the Department of Labor's revised fiduciary rule proposal for more brokers under the Obama administration. Aside from creating the immediate confusion within the wealth management industry, it would have potentially put many brokers who were not already fiduciaries out of business or forced to reduce offerings to clients. Once the Trump administration came along, the proposal was eliminated.

Nevertheless, the back and forth of the regulatory uncertainty wreaked havoc for several years on many financial professionals. To sum things up, regulatory bodies and governmental power brokers are not exempt from perpetrating fraud or using aggressive and unethical tactics to achieve an end for their own purposes at the expense of your client-advisor relationship. The best way to handle this particular conundrum is to work with your broker nimbly by permitting them the means to adjust your investment strategy for the long term when regulators throw curveballs or poison the soup with acid, so to speak.

Broker Fraud or Attorney Fraud—Discern the Difference

One area that can be problematic for a client or investor is being able to discern the true reputation of a wealth manager. For those paying any attention to business or financial news, it's not hard to find evidence of wrongdoing by a wealth manager. Stories abound of financial advisors who stole their clients' funds for personal use, such as luxury yachts or vacations. It's often commonly heard also how some brokers trade within clients' accounts or shuffle funds among accounts without a client's permission. So how can an investor, who may not have the time to investigate such wrongdoing, should it occur in their own portfolio, know if they are dealing with an honest broker? Well, the answer can get complicated since there are two sides to the story.

Statement verification and churning

There are several things an investor can do to understand if they are dealing with a broker who knows how to be fair, compliant, and ethical. First, a client should always check their monthly statements to look for purchases or sales of investment positions that were not approved by the client or may be for an amount that was not proportional or agreed to relative to the stated trading objectives when the relationship first began.

Another item to look out for on the statements is to see if your account number changes. This situation may not be as obvious as the first. Every once in a while, a custodian firm may need to change technology suites for their platform and, as a result, new account numbers may be issued for the same account you have always held with the firm. There would be nothing unusual with this if it only happens once every several years or decade. What is more suspicious is when your account numbers change within a year's time when you did not request any additional services or changes to your account as a client. What this could be an indication of is the unethical, illegal, and immoral practice of churning accounts.

Churning, in reference to securities and account trading, is defined as the frequent rotation, creation, or purchasing and selling of accounts or investment products at a fast pace with no benefit to the client or investor. This practice is illegal and should be brought to the attention of someone who can assess the situation. Usually, the assessor would be the principal, branch manager, or compliance department of your advisor's affiliated firm. In the most conspicuous cases that came to the attention of the mass media, large firms were even pressuring employees and advisors to open up new accounts in clients' names without their knowledge or approval. Obviously, these are very egregious examples of advisor misconduct that can affect an investor's wealth and possibly even their reputation or credit score. However, attempts at fraud or misconduct are not merely one directional. Many times in the industry, financial advisors or brokerage firms become victims of fraud perpetrated against them by attorneys or unethical clients.

Legal extortion

To explain, a little backdrop needs to be offered. Given the large sums of money that financial advisors and the wealth management field deal with, they naturally become targets of unscrupulous attorneys looking for a big payday. With the structure of the financial system's regulatory system, attorneys and many clients realize that all they need to do to secure a big payout is to make a false claim, bring it to the attention of the regulatory bodies like FINRA or the SEC, and then wait for a mediation or arbitration panel to commence. This is one way that financial industry professionals fall prey to and essentially become cash cows for attorneys and their immoral clients looking to extort advisors and firms.

Such attorneys realize that it is more cost effective for a large firm, such as a bank or wire house, to simply offer a settlement payout in short amounts of time under a year to make the claim go away than it would be for the firm to fight it and prove no wrongdoing. Therefore, even though no wrong may have been done by the advisor or firm, they can still often be left with a blemish on their record due to the inefficiency or cost of trying to remove the fraudulent claim from their record.

Background checks

When a client begins a new relationship with a financial advisor, there are basically two resources the client can look at to determine if the advisor or firm has any significant claims against them that warrant caution. FINRA's BrokerCheck system and the SEC's IARD system both give assessments of an advisor's history. Both of these resources were briefly discussed earlier in the book. As a client, when looking through these records, it is important to understand that many claims or disclosures can easily be false or of little significance.

For instance, an advisor might have a small tax lien liability from many years ago that was never removed from the record. Or there could be a negative remark about communications, marketing, or advertisement. These kinds of matters should bear little weight on your decision to work with any given advisor. Such blemishes are common on many advisors' records. That's not to say I am trying to be an apologist for such records, but it is to say that many fraudulent or minor claims continually find their way on to advisors' and firms' regulatory records each year as ever aggressive regulators, fraudulent attorneys and unethical consumers try to milk the industry for as much money as they can get from it.

One little known tidbit that is not commonly known to the general public but generally understood within financial advisor circles is that, eventually, almost every financial advisor or wealth manager will have a major claim, be it true or false, brought against their practice. As a general rule of thumb, if an advisor has been in practice for at least between seven and ten years, then the majority of those advisors will have had a false claim brought against them that they had to defend and disprove. And what's more, from my own perspective of practice and all the other financial advisors I have known through my career who have been in the business ten years or more, most of them have had major claims filed against them.

As the continuous turnstile of false claims are brought through the regulatory agencies each year, a client should understand that many of the claims that may show up on a financial advisor's record will be removed in a matter of time. Through an expungement process available through the regulatory agencies, financial advisors can usually have false claims removed from their records within an average amount of time, perhaps between two and five years. From the point of view of the client, what's important to look out for is any claims that were settled or paid out for a large sum that are still on an advisor's record for over six years. If the claim stays on an advisor's record when there was a large sum of money involved, then it may be an indicator that the advisor did actually do something wrong that needed to be atoned for. But just as important, a client should not give much weight to any claims on an advisor's record within three years of the current date. Many of these claims will be removed from the record as the advisor successfully shows to the regulators that they were fraudulent claims by former clients or unethical attorneys.

From my own experience, even I have had to defend against a fraudulent claim that was brought against me. The claim was easily proved to be fraudulent and subsequently removed from my record, but it just goes to show how easy it is for anyone trying to extort financial industry professionals to easily make the attempt. To make matters worse, the regulatory bodies have even considered in recent years some new rule proposals that would make it virtually impossible for an advisor to disprove and remove a fraudulent claim against their record. Although it has not become regulation yet as of the date of this book's writing, many regulators want to completely eliminate the expungement process for financial advisors. In other words, they want to take away even the ability for a financial advisor to defend themselves and show that the claims were fraudulent.

Whatever your opinion or view of the financial industry may be, I can definitely say, in my own opinion, that this prospective rule sounds much more like establishing kangaroo courts as opposed to due process or justice being served. Fortunately, this egregious imbalance toward processing of hearings and justice has not taken hold, at least not yet. Should such a proposed regulation actually become implemented, it would mean it could be nearly impossible for any client to find an advisor with a clean record, making the process of deciding who to work with even more cumbersome or unclear.

An exploitative business model

For you as a novice investor, what's important to know is that some attorneys structure entire business models around trying to defame or extort financial advisors by trying to induce either unethical or unaware clients into making false claims for big paydays. Typically, many of these unethical and extortive law firms tend to congregate in a few states. While you can find examples of unethical attorneys everywhere, there are a few places where such practices are more prevalent than others. The highest concentration of such types of practices tend to structure themselves in the most populous states with large concentrations of ultrahigh-net-worth individuals. New York, California, Florida, and Illinois, where state statutes more easily enable such immoral practices, appear to have more than their fair share of such law firms, from my own observations and personal experience.

Hopefully, as an investor, you are not of the mindset to try to employ such immoral tactics for the purpose of extorting financial professionals. Just be aware that, especially today with the ubiquity of information on the internet, attorneys constantly and wrongly try to associate advisors or firms with bad behavior by posting misleading or blatantly false information about those advisors or firms. Their hope is to find someone naive enough to go along with their scheme to file a fraudulent claim.

In reality, when claims are successful in the mediation or arbitration process, the paid-out amount usually only comes to 10 percent or less of the actual original amount claimed. And more often than not, the claims are found to be misleading to the point where nothing is paid out to the claimant. So to summarize, it is very important for an investor to know that attorney fraud occurs equally as much as advisor fraud and that the aforementioned rules of thumb can help to at least give you a minimal understanding of what is important on an advisor's record versus what is not. Knowing the difference can help offer you a little more peace of mind in knowing that you are dealing with an ethical financial advisor who is truly there to serve you through fiduciary obligations.

Caller, You're <u>Not</u> on the Line!

Since the wealth management industry is so fraught with false claims against advisors and firms, a client may rightfully ask how this could impact his or her working with a financial advisor. The answer is simple. Many firms' compliance departments are so wary of litigation and obsessed with protecting reputation that they impose strict guidelines on their financial advisors regarding exactly how much communication they should have with an individual client. So if you're wondering why you don't hear very often from your financial advisor or if you feel you are always having to initiate contact when you would like more proactive outreach from them, here are several reasons why.

The advisor's muzzle

Internally held and what is not often revealed to new clients is that many of the large wire houses or banks maintain general guidelines for frequency of contact with a client. For instance, if a client has less than $500,000 in assets held with a firm, a firm's upper management may suggest the advisor only call that client once or twice per year to satisfy regulatory obligations. Given that the majority of retail investors have less than this amount, it is no wonder the majority of investors don't hear much from their brokers. Sadly, the majority of many financial advisors' time gets spent on talking to the clients with the most assets in an advisor's book. From my own experience, I can attest to how little attention I received when I was a client before.

I used to practice full time as an architect before entering the wealth management profession. As a retail investing client during my years as an architect, I held my brokerage accounts with one of the largest wire houses in the country, which is a household name. In over ten years of being a client with them, the professional who was serving as my broker proactively reached out to me three times at most. Only three times in ten years. What's worse is the last time he reached out to me was to invite me to a dinner seminar for the primary purpose of his soliciting new assets through my personal connections for his book of business. That doesn't exactly fit my idea of putting a client's interests first. Needless to say, my confidence in that firm's abilities to serve me as client took a major hit; after which, I decided I could do a better job with my knowledge of finance to serve clients better than I was served.

Big brother compliance

Additionally, many large firms' compliance operations will even go so far as to equip themselves with acute monitoring of every single e-mail that passes through an office on a daily basis. The computer search programs that are utilized scan every single e-mail for trigger words that a firm's legal or compliance department deem problematic or able to increase liability. Such programs come in handy to ensure that financial advisors do not make inappropriate statements, such as guaranteeing security performance or making future projections. On the other hand, sometimes, firms will take the effort to the extremes and essentially start operating like the nazi gestapo to control every opportunity for a financial advisor to speak with their clients or prospects.

This is another reason why many advisors fail to take the initiative to reach out to their clients more often. The sometimes overly heavy hand of big brother does tend to rear its head at larger firms. A good rule of thumb for a new investor would be to reach out to your financial advisor at least twice a year if he does not initiate contact already that often. Doing so will allow your advisor to verify changes to your life and review whether changes to your portfolio or investment strategy should be made at the time of those calls.

One of the primary reasons I chose to write *Traps of Treasure* is for the general benefit of new investors, both young and old, who have not had much experience to guide them on a path forward through the brokerage world. Looking back, I wish someone could have been there to guide me or give me broad swaths of information to show me how to avoid pitfalls when working with a financial advisor. Although I was already very knowledgeable regarding the market and knew how to trade from an early age, I was not well versed in the immaterial and internal matters to the wealth management world that affect relationships and, hence, portfolio performance or retirement planning.

Had I known the information I know today regarding the internal mechanics and relationship meandering within the financial world, I might have been able to save a lot of time with my own wealth management plan. With any luck and understanding, the information in this book can at least clear much of the fog on the road ahead for you when you initiate a relationship with a financial professional.

CHAPTER 6

I Will Not Set Before My Eyes Anything That Is Worthless
Media Manipulations

So let's talk about the media in its numerous forms. Much blame is laid upon the media in our society today, rightfully so, for blatantly presenting either one-sided or divisive commentary that is unapologetically biased. And all sides of an argument are to blame for this. Growing up, we are educated that one of the purposes of journalism is to present an objective and unbiased gathering of facts from which people can then make their own judgments. However, with the current state of society and media operations, the opportunity to make critical judgments for oneself based on presented information has become all but impossible.

It seems today that all media outlets only present stories with one-sided information or prevent objective assessment by censoring certain documents, videos, or evidence that could alter the debate of an issue. And from everything I've seen over the past several years, especially with the unchecked growth of social media and its censorship capabilities, it appears this situation is not going to correct itself anytime soon. Therefore, if a consumer or investor is not able to rely upon media outlets for accurate information, how can an investor or someone starting their journey toward retirement make correct assessments of situations that may affect their long-term investing horizon? In this chapter, I will lay out several approaches that an investor can use to help guide them when making decisions for their financial well-being.

What would you do for thirty pieces of silver? As the Scriptures tell us, Judas provided information and sold out his Savior for a small amount of money, the thirty pieces of silver. Much to his detriment, Judas discovered that his gain for betrayal was a worthless reward. In a similar fashion, media outlets garner vast sums of money by way of spreading false, biased, or manipulated data and by spreading unverified hearsay. So in essence, most media outlets are relying on the fact that most consumers will not take the time to verify any information presented to them due to lack of time or interest. Thereby, they easily garner vast profits through subscriptions and renewals while essentially providing nothing of material value that can improve your lot in life with clear information on how to invest or save.

As a new investor or client, it is absolutely imperative that you learn how to prevent worthless information from being presented before your eyes. The inability to decipher fake information can be destructive to your wealth management plan because it could lead you to make impulsive decisions based on speculative information or rumor that does not pan out to be true. Those impulsive decisions, when executed at the wrong time during market cycles, can leave a portfolio devastated with losses that could take many years to recover, if at all. Remember, media outlets use continuous psychological strategies through clickbait, the structural framing of their websites, ad positioning, and artificial intelligence-targeted programming of responses to lure you in to their web. Avoid it at all costs when considering anything related to finance.

The Headline Du Jour: Media Mania

Part of your financial advisor's job is to discern for you the impact of certain events and data upon your investments and retirement plans. They will perform this function with great attention to detail, at least the high-quality advisors in the profession will. And usually, they will rely on a few select sources of information upon which they rely. Many times, those sources of information will be internal data from the analysts within their firms, which are less prone to media manipulation.

Internal information

Such data is usually a highly chart-oriented and numbers-gathering exercise to assess raw information for the current state of affairs in a given sector of the market, company, or economic data from governmental agencies. And often, this information will be only for internal use of the financial advisor, not to be disseminated to the general public or the advisor's clients. If a financial advisor is independent or does not work for a large bank or wire house that provides such internal information, then they will often subscribe to a third-party provider of economic and market data that they trust, of which there are many sources.

One item to ask of your financial advisor specifically is to find out exactly what his sources of data are for the investment recommendations he makes. If that information is available for disclosure to the general public, then you, as a client, should ask if you can receive access to that same information to follow along with your advisor's thought process. Coming to assessments together with your advisor using the same data can ease the pressure of the relationship and make working with a financial advisor much easier.

Unreliable data

One of the biggest mistakes that I personally see with almost every client is the client's attempt to do their own research from biased or unreliable sources found on the internet or paid subscriptions. The client will then bring their own assessment to the table, which may be in conflict with the tedious research the financial advisor does, and interject the client's own trading instructions for their accounts. This is probably one of the biggest errors a client can make when working with a financial advisor. A financial advisor meticulously plans out an investment strategy that requires consistent application over many years to succeed. It is the primary function of a client to approve or disapprove of that strategy and the products presented to you by your financial advisor. When a client brings outside information and interjects it into that strategy, the competing ideas may be incompatible and can have negative effects on a portfolio.

The other significant mistake that new clients, and even investors with many years of trading experience, make is falling into the temptation of being led by daily headlines of market news sources. With over ten years practicing as a private wealth manager, and over twenty-five years of steadily observing market data, I can definitely say without hesitation that easily over 90 percent of everything that is posted on investment news outlets is useless fluff or repeated material from past publication cycles. The first trap I have found that many investors get lured into is the repeated back and forth, on a daily basis, of presentation of opposing viewpoints of market predictions. For example, one day, a market news outlet will post an article about the impending correction about to happen in the markets and that investors should put their money predominantly into cash. The very next day, that same news outlet will post an article in direct contradiction to this by saying that the market is about to start a new upward cycle and that investors should quickly buy positions to take advantage of the coming gains.

As an advisor myself, it is my job to pay attention to such news outlets to be informed of what my clients are seeing and how they could potentially be swayed. Admittedly, though, I have never given any credence at all to any of the articles posted on the market news outlets. My preference has always been to look at raw numerical data from multiple sources, which can then be compared against one another, and then develop my own opinions to help guide my clients in building a wealth management plan for them. From the constant daily back and forth of contradictory material, it is not hard to see how a client or new investor could become confused. My recommendation would be to turn off the market news and only look at it on an infrequent basis if you are compelled to do so as a client. In the long run, your stress levels and worrying over clickbait will decrease, and you will be no worse off for it, having spent the saved time on other efforts in your life.

Recycled headlines

Another manipulative feature of investment news outlets is their act of recycling past articles and opinion pieces from previous quarters or years. It would be much less profitable for news outlets to have to constantly create new reading content every single day. Therefore, as a more efficient method to make money, they will frequently modify the headlines or make minor changes to past articles then repost them to fill the pages of their sites or publications. The unethical behavior behind this methodology of media outlets lies in the fact that many times, the reposted material will no longer be relevant to the actual market conditions of the day it is republished. Or maybe the economic cycle is not at the appropriate position in its present cycle for the article to be germane. Altogether, this practice of dusting off old opinion pieces or articles and reposting them at a later date can be deceptive to the general investment public.

Not being aware of the true relevance of daily posted market news could induce a client to make incorrect and impulsive decisions for their wealth management plan when, in fact, the reality of the present economic situation may be different from the information that was presented in the article. The trap of falling prey to outdated media disinformation is ever present. As people, we are all psychologically prone to being seduced or drawn in by new information or at least what we perceive to be new information. The reality is that most of what is thrown about in market media outlets is just rehash or placed in rotation, like a radio station DJ revolving albums and songs through the days of the week on a radio station.

Sourcing your own data

If you are the kind of investor who prefers the do-it-yourself way and wants to go it alone with an online trading platform to manage your own portfolio, I would suggest that you find one or two data sources that could be used consistently each week and month through the years. The consistent flow of data from one or two reliable sources will help you filter out opinion prognosticators and you will eventually be able to see a rhythm to the reporting cycles that you can be accustomed to over several years. Consistency is key in this approach. And it would not be wise to switch among various data sources since it may cause an investor to second-guess their convictions when their plan may have been solid and correct in the first place.

And as a matter of practice, I will say that I have never paid any attention to any opinion articles discussing economic or product data. Please note the difference that while *Traps of Treasure* may be my own personal opinion writing about the internal operations of the wealth management industry and how to avoid its pitfalls, the book does not opine over any specific investments or product data. Over the course of my entire career, I have never found one article from an opinion writer that discusses specific investment products to be useful in any way, shape, or form. Once again, I have always considered these types of articles to be superfluous attention grabbers. It could be better to obtain raw data from prospectuses, white sheets, and quarterly reports. These documents are essentially summary sheets or pamphlets provided by fund or product companies on a regular schedule. Such documents go through an approval and compliance process first through regulators or internal firm compliance departments.

Beware of the daily headlines since they can imprint within your mind a repeatable pattern of addiction to seeking out new information that you may wonder if it is relevant to your investment situation. Instead, rely on, or allow your financial advisor to provide, raw numerical data, such as quarterly earnings reports, trend line charts of the indexes or positions you invest in, and quarterly governmental reports to help you make decisions about your investments. These forms of data are published less frequently and won't keep you futilely chasing the same information like a cat chasing a red dot across the living room from its owner's laser pointer. Put more simply, turn off the noise from the daily investment media outlets, and keep it turned off.

Life is too short to waste it on manipulated presentations biased one way or another. You'll enjoy life more if you rely on your financial advisor for such data and if you keep your eyes away from the glaring headlines. Don't forget, the media is relying upon you to help support their garnishing their thirty pieces of silver for themselves. They do this by luring you in with sensationalist headlines meant to induce people to impulsively react on a frequent basis. It's better to invest your money than give it to the media who will not offer you anything of material tangible value in return.

Stop Chasing the Hot Dot!

Separate from the manipulations of daily headlines, another trap that new investors can fall into is what is colloquially called within the wealth management industry as "chasing the hot dot." As one of the worst habits an investor can develop, trying to chase what appears to be the hot commodity of the day or trying to find the best-performing money manager based on the most recent returns tends to be a losing game. In addition, not being able to recognize when investment trends become overbought by too many people tends to add to the frustration and detriment of a planned-out investment strategy. We'll take a look at these ideas right now.

Building and culling the herd

One of the worst habits of the media is to try to put forth and promote a single security or commodity where everyone and their uncle seem to be getting in on the action. These individual securities have many times been technology related over the past twenty or thirty years. Once the position attains a little traction and word of mouth on Wall Street, it begins to garner attention from a small but critical following of institutional investors. Then as the position starts to grab more attention, it eventually makes its way to the media headlines where it becomes ripe for the picking among even more institutional investors. And then as a last act, the media attention and notoriety begin to reach the attention of the mass retail investment crowd. This pattern of building up a small yet relatively new security to overvalued levels in a few years creates a precarious position.

Those who aren't watching can succumb to a sudden and dramatic fall in the position's market price and valuation. Essentially, what happens is that the overvaluation of the security was not justified by its actual value to consumers. Rather, the inflating of the price allows a few savvy but unethical investors, who may have information not afforded to the general public, to harvest the gains while remaining investors are left to watch the security plummet and lose value. This practice, by the way, is an illegal one. But unfortunately, it happens more often than the general public may suspect and with continued frequency throughout the years.

Initial public offerings (IPOs) that are offered by large banks and wire houses commonly become the vessels of this kind of practice, in addition to many new start-up biomedical or technology companies. In a few instances, the skyrocketing prices of such positions do truly stand the test of time and become highly regarded companies. But more often is the case that such companies do not. Therefore, a new investor should not start salivating at the thought of making big bucks by chasing the hot dot of what appears to be the latest and hottest security promoted by the media. If you do, you may just end up feeling like you got burned.

Nascent performance memory

The other danger for new investors is seduction by a fund or portfolio manager's most recent returns. Simply put, no advisor or money manager bats a thousand over the course of his career. All managers make incorrect calls just as much as they make stellar calls when it comes to investment strategy. One misperception that is commonly portrayed in the media is the habit of media outlets to tout the incredible returns of a specific fund or money manager. They may say that the manager beat the market by a whopping 10 percent, 20 percent, 30 percent, 40 percent, or whatever return serves their sensationalist agenda. And it is true, over the course of career, many managers will have that one spectacular year where they made all the right calls at the right times to create evidence of an outrageously successful portfolio performance during a single given year or during a very volatile time during the market cycle. The problem with this is that such outstanding results are very rarely replicated to the same level by the same manager in subsequent years.

Market rotation occurs among sectors, regulations change, and other variables come into focus that make the secret ingredients to that previous stellar performance unrepeatable. The media will continue to rotate their star managers that they want to promote through their monthly or yearly headlines. But the plain truth is that either those managers are reserved only for ultrahigh-net-worth investors or that those managers will fail to perform for you in the years after they had their one hit wonder. A simpler approach, if you choose to work with third-party fund or money managers, would be to seek out funds or portfolio managers who have a long and consistent track record of growth. Those fund managers may not offer an eye-popping rate of return to exaggerate, but at least you'll have the comfort of knowing they can provide stability, consistency, and a methodized framework for achieving future returns based on past experience.

These are some of the refrains I see repeated time and time again in the media regarding market cycles: "But this time, it truly is different" or "The new normal." More often than not, I have found these statement to be the famous last words of a market prognosticator who is in denial of current market circumstances and who is desperately clinging to a wrong but dearly held conviction he can't let go of. We could look at a case study example of how this plays out.

Roller-coaster parabolas

The year 2017 produced phenomenal gains across the broad spectrum of the market. It cyclically favored a passive over active management strategy. The last market correction that occurred prior to these gains was in January of 2016, leading to uninterrupted growth with only minor dips of nothing more than 3 percent. But from a technical standpoint, the produced gains became definitively parabolic. As asset prices increase, their charts show an exponentially increasing rise in upward curvature. This had been the case for the major indices as well as for Bitcoin, to call out a specific example. Multiple hedge funds began preparing to short Bitcoin as it became a tradeable futures contract. This could have been a telling indicator of the future direction of Bitcoin itself as well as the broader market.

The problem with upwardly explosive asset behavior, as history repeatedly proves, is that such increases in short time also produce massive drops that can mirror the rise by the same amount or more. Bitcoin's charts exemplified how far parabolic charts can extend upward in dramatic fashion. Technology, fashion, and investment products change at an astonishingly fast pace. Yet human behavior and psychology remain consistent. The tempting nature to jump on the bubble bandwagon to avoid being left out can create a fear sentiment, often leading to impulsive decisions and reckless investment strategies. This behavioral cycle repeats decade after decade after decade and so on, with no end in sight.

A more prudent response to such market or product behavior is to choose not to buy into the platitude refrain oft proclaimed high on a mountaintop by others that the current bull run in that product will keep going. Promoters of the product will then say, "This time, the increase is truly different from past market run-ups" or "It can continue to sustain itself for the foreseeable future." On the contrary, newly formed product bubbles will eventually pop just as easily as past market bubbles did even though no one can pinpoint which week it will occur or which event will trigger the drop.

As is often said, "All good things must come to an end." When markets or individual securities rise significantly over very short periods of time, it would be advisable to keep an eye on the bigger picture of long-term investing by focusing on asset and gains protection. From my own convictions as a wealth manager, I chose to avoid the cryptocurrencies and media sensation surrounding them until they could be properly regulated and tied to hard assets. To the contrary, all I saw from the media and promoters of the products was the tired refrain and behavior of "It keeps going up, so let's join the crowd."

Eventually, Bitcoin took a hard fall by the beginning of 2018, and a lot of investors lost money from the mania, just as money fallen prey to by past schemes in prior decades. With the passing of every five to ten years, it seems that these pump-and-dump schemes seem to fade from collective memory and the mass subconsciousness. Then, after enough time, history repeats itself with a new investment product fad, only to have more people lose money and be disappointed once again.

All in all, it is tempting for the novice investor to be attracted to the novelty of the products, platforms, and research available with easy access to the web. However, the most successful portfolios and strategies I've seen always understood that the noise coming from the headlines really only serve as a distraction to be avoided. That noise can be more of an impediment to the necessary focus of implementing a long-term plan. To say it easiest, it's better to save your money and time than waste it on worthless things laid out before your eyes on a silver platter.

CHAPTER 7

Theories of Relativity
Misunderstandings and Misrepresentations

Looking at your neighbors or your peers, have you ever wondered why they always seem to be doing so much better than you financially, professionally, or otherwise? Many in our society fall into the trap of trying to keep up with the Joneses at some point in their lives, especially during the child-rearing years and during midlife. The seven deadly sins continue to find a way to try to creep in to our lives. Pride, envy, greed, lust, anger, gluttony, and sloth are relentless in trying to hinder our efforts toward salvation. And where money and finances are concerned, envy and greed seem to be the most pertinent of the seven.

Look closer behind the patina, and you'll see something less than attractive when comparing yourself to others. Under the facade of high-end luxury vehicles, extravagant home remodeling, frequent trips to exotic locations, and other amenities lies a disturbing truth—that much of that apparent wealth is financed with debt or by using cash flow methods of kicking the can down the road. These methods of sustaining a lavish lifestyle usually fail as they are unsustainable over the long haul. They are psychological manipulations meant to distract people from more pragmatic means to building wealth and a creating a solid foundation for retirement. That solid foundation can then afford you the ability to have the freedoms you want to live the life you desire unhindered by the stress of having to work for a paycheck instead of wanting to work for personal interest.

Several ways that new investors fall into traps and become tricked by misrepresentations are the following. Many people with technical backgrounds often assume investing is easy. They will think that simply opening up an account on a low-cost online trading platform and finding their own research through the online investment blogs will give them access to the inner circle of the investment world. Much to their chagrin, they later discover that their lack of success or losses in their investment accounts resulted from disinformation provided over the internet.

Another way in which new investors fall into psychological traps is by developing a fear of missing out relative to their colleagues, who always seem to be talking about the successes of their investment portfolios. In reality, most of what is claimed by colleagues tends to be hyperbole that should not be given any credence whatsoever. And another failure to recognize objective assessments is by looking at very-high-net-worth individuals and billionaires or industry titans and guessing how the wealth was produced.

Each of these misunderstandings create a negative feedback loop in the mind of any investor and merely distract them from focusing on their own individual path to financial success. Moral teachings probably explain it best in saying that greed and envy will only deter you from happiness. I could not say it better, so let's now take a closer look at detailed ways to avoid falling into these traps as new investors or clients.

Investing Is Easy—That's Why Everyone Is a Multimillionaire

As mentioned previously in the book, wealth management was not my first career. I began my professional efforts with a degree in civil engineering, a very technical background to say the least, with a lot of emphasis on calculation, economics, statistics, and other studies directly applicable to finance. Upon completing that, I then pursued my first creative interest endeavor and became licensed as an architect, of which I am still licensed to this day. Needless to say, my path to the world of investing and providing advice to others as a financial advisor was a long and roundabout route. But along the way, I discovered in many of my peers an inability to objectively understand various underpinnings of investing.

Professional reprogramming

To clarify, I followed the path of an engineer in the beginning of my professional studies. Twenty years later, hindsight has shown me the effect various distinct professional mindsets have had on the lives of many of my former collegiate colleagues. Every profession has unique but often divergent ways of essentially programming its members' way of thinking to solve problems and create solutions for the real world. For instance, many of my college peers went on to become professionally licensed engineers. Given the extensive and exceptional technical background engineers develop over the course of their studies, many engineers believe they can simply apply their knowledge to the investment markets and do their own investing for themselves through a do-it-yourself trading platform online. The error and misunderstanding of this belief lies in thinking that mathematical application of market analysis alone is adequate to succeed in making money.

In a sense, the problem of pride rears its ugly head in thinking one knows more than they actually do regarding an endeavor. Technical understanding alone is not sufficient to create a well-rounded and stable financial base. The other major component that is often overlooked by engineers, but which is essential to successfully navigating the markets, is the psychological behavior of the market, which can't always be quantified. Both understandings are vitally important to creating and protecting a wealth management plan. Yet I still see many engineers, accountants, economists, and technology professionals who slave away working eighty hours or more per week without reaping the fruit of their harvest in any significant way. The lack of ability to acknowledge mass psychology's equal importance to technical comprehension often hinders success in investment planning.

The physician's syndrome

Physicians and medical professionals are another example of highly skilled professionals who often do not meet their investment objectives or major life goals. One may think that with the very high salaries that medical professionals make relative to the rest of the population, they would have an easy time saving for retirement and building a solid financial foundation. That thought is often far from the truth. Unlike engineers, physicians and medical field professionals encounter their own distinct roadblocks to financial security and peace of mind.

Most of us are familiar with the high entry cost for physicians to their profession due to education loans. And many of us understand, or at least empathize with, the grueling schedules and workload of medical residencies, never-ending patient loads, or the ever-present risk of medical malpractice litigation. For medical professionals, misunderstanding of the operation of the investing world is not so much a lack of technical or psychological understanding. Rather, it is often an inability to grasp the scope of their relative earnings toward the cost of being in their profession. Put in simpler terms, what good is working grueling hours and making vast sums of money if the quality of life suffers because you are not permitted adequate time to spend with your family or on your personal endeavors.

Relationships sometimes fail as a result or stress loads become so overwhelming that it manifests itself through physical ailments for the doctor. Even when medical professionals achieve an extensive amount of personal wealth, they may often continue with such grueling workloads well beyond an age where necessary. This may be because they have become so accustomed to it that they can't envision any other mode of living. Or, rather, it might simply be greed.

Regardless, financial advisors will often encounter such professionals who are essentially hostages to fortune and cannot find a way out to a better life. This is where the financial advisor comes in and can be of great assistance. A financial advisor can offer an objective perspective to many professionals by assessing the balance in a client's life among money, time, relationships, and mental stress. Many professionals fall into a myopic misunderstanding that just because their modus operandi of life has operated one way for so many years, it can't be changed. On the contrary, it can be changed. Many times, people just need an outside observer to recognize it for them and show them how to change.

Whatever your individual profession may be, the plain fact of the matter is that investing and mapping out a stable strategy for retirement is hard. If it were easy, as touted by many professionals who have technical backgrounds, many more people would be multimillionaires. But they aren't. As a new investor, it is important that you come to the wealth management world and approach toward investing with a clearly open mind and no preconceived notions about the methods that may be used to help you achieve your goals.

If you are the kind of person who enjoys doing your own research and injecting your own investment analysis in a discussion with your financial professional, then by all means do so. It will help your advisor get a clearer understanding of your thought process. At the same time, don't worry or take it too personally if your own ideas are not corroborated by a professional. Wealth planning is an extremely complicated puzzle with many individual parts. Not all parts are meant to go together as easily as a jigsaw puzzle.

I Have This Friend Who—

Moving on to another major misunderstanding is the severe mistake of taking unverified information from a colleague or friend and assuming it to be gospel where investing is concerned. If I had a penny for every time a client, colleague, or friend informed me of some rate of return that they or their friend achieved by investing in a certain product or using some method, I would be contently retired. As an advisor, what I have personally discovered is that every single one of those statements was either false or was never corroborated with proof, such as a monthly statements or performance reports.

As a new investor, be sure to understand that such statements are nothing more than mental manipulations meant as an attempt to give the person who is saying them a mental advantage over you. Pay absolutely no attention to such statements.

The unproven returns

Another ploy and trick in this scenario is when someone might have actually made a good return on a specific product or over a certain period of time. Yet what they might not be showing you is the whole performance of all their accounts. Let's say for example that a person made 20 percent gain in an account for a year, and he could even prove it with statements. Well, that might be great, but he could also be refraining from telling you about his other brokerage or retirement accounts that might have been down 10 percent that year. Depending upon the size of the different account and the weighted averages of the performance, his gains might be nothing more than flat for the year.

Never make a decision for your own accounts and never make any adjustments to your investment strategy based on hearsay from a friend. It is one of the quickest and easiest ways to derail your plan and cause harm to your long-term asset growth. Above and beyond that, your financial advisor, if you work with one, will already be able to recognize that the statement is most likely hot air and false embellishment on the part of your colleague who made the claim. No statement should ever be taken to be held true without exact and timely reporting. Rather, a new client should rely on the regulated reports that are provided by companies and monthly and annual statements or recent quantifiable data about specific investment products put forth by an established third-party reporting company.

In my tenure as a wealth manager, no one has ever proved or corroborated any proof of substantial or enormous gains from their own personal accounts with proof from multiple time frame statements when I asked them for detailed data so I could perform a comparative analysis. Not once. Of course, new clients and prospects will come to me with their current account statements when they ask for my help to analyze or if they are thinking of working with me.

What I refer to are often proclaimed but never substantiated vague statements of hitting the jackpot meant to induce you to look into a colleague's way of thinking or doing things. Always beware that such statements are usually just self-aggrandizing attempts for someone to say, "Look what I have" or "Look what I did" or "Look what you don't have" or "Look what you didn't do." It is nothing more than a ruse to be completely ignored. In fact, if someone makes such statements to you, you may want to question the credibility of other remarks they make even outside of the realm of finance.

The Enclaves versus the Other 95 Percent

One last area of misrepresentation and misunderstanding is how each of us views ourselves relative to the concentrated wealth of others we may see in the media. One of the worst manifestations of this came about in the eighties and nineties with the television show *Lifestyles of the Rich and Famous*. For those who remember it, it's not a far stretch to say that the main purpose of the show was to indirectly and subtly make those who could not achieve such excessive wealth feel less than successful. However, so many years later, it might be a fun exercise to investigate exactly how many of the wealthy individuals on that show were eventually legally prosecuted or even convicted for the means and methods by which they achieved such excesses.

The concentrated enclaves of wealth, such as the Hamptons, West Palm Beach, Southern California, Marin County, and North Dallas, will always be there to portray an unattainable level of wealth that can only be achieved by roughly 5 percent of the population through media, technology, medicine, entertainment, and professional sports ventures. Or if the wealth didn't come by way of one of those paths, odds are likely that it is simply unearned inheritance. For the other 95 percent of the population who has to employ methods of creating financial sustainability on a monthly or yearly basis throughout our whole lives, the important thing to remember is to focus on a more realistic and quantifiable goal that can be broken down over time.

Break down your time frames

A good way to do this would be to break down the entire anticipated time frame of your life into one-, five-, and ten-year blocks. When looking at those blocks, start to write down specific monetary targets that you would like to achieve that are realistic as a percentage of your annual take-home salary. Whether you make $30,000 per year or $300,000 per year, a plan can always be implemented to isolate and prioritize your long-term financial security. What's even more important is not to live beyond your means by throwing hard-earned money away toward items, events, or situations that do not offer long-term tangible appreciation. Entertainment is one of the areas where much wealth can be quickly and easily lost without even recognizing it. The additional appetizers and drinks that we all like to order when we go out to eat at a restaurant also become little assassins over time that draw our personal savings down.

It's in the little things where the rot begins. Therefore, when working with your financial advisor, it is imperative that, together, you both analyze every minute expenditure you incur on a weekly and even daily basis. The incremental savings will not help you to become an ultrahigh-net-worth individual or millionaire, but they will help to prevent you from creating an unsustainable financial situation in the future when stormy weather approaches in your life. Define very specific, tangible, and realistic goals throughout each decade of your life and even more frequent than that. The discipline to stay focused on those goals will help divert your attention away from the unrealistic ideals achieved by the few who had access to very lucrative business models from a very young age.

Comparison conundrum

Remember, there is no better vision for your life than the one you laid out for yourself when you were young. Playing the comparison game draws you further away from your original intents with each passing year. Additionally, it is just as important to recognize one's own professional situation in life. Not all professions are created equal nor is pay for valued time. Another trick is not to place unrealistic expectations on yourself or your financial advisor if investment contributions may be limited. Significant growth of an investment portfolio also requires the ability to compound. And compounding needs one of either two things—an infusion of cash or time—ideally both at the same time to work in conjunction.

All in all, don't fall prey to any of the traps of relative comparison. At the end of the day, what matters most in investing is that you achieved the maximum attainable reward for your efforts and that you enjoy the fruits of your labors. Extravagant lifestyles, comparisons to other professionals' ways of life, and distractions caused by disinformation should all be suppressed in your mind as you venture out on your way to working with a financial professional to create your plan and strategy.

Wasting time wishing for things you most likely will never have or wondering why imbalances in social equity aren't tackled on a large scale will only slow you down in your progress. Don't be too hard on yourself when strategies don't go as planned while investing. And don't assume your successes are always due to your own innovation or intellectual acumen. A little humility and introspection now and then can be very useful tools to keep you focused and objective toward reaching those dreams you had when you were young.

CHAPTER 8

Moving Goalposts
The Industry's Continuous Reinvention

One thing that gets lost over a twenty-, thirty-, or forty-year investment time horizon is the fact that nothing remains the same in the world of finance. Like any fashion trend of clothing, cars, entertainment, or housing, the products and structure of wealth management are created, rotated, and eventually become overmarketed to the point that they no longer provide reasonable gains after time. Because of this cyclical rotation, industry professionals and companies need to reinvent themselves and their branding every decade or so. If they didn't do so, the general investing public would lose interest in their products, and profits would decrease.

Being a new investor or client, you need to be aware of such rotational patterns so that you don't fall behind the curve, so to speak, and are left with underperforming products that do not keep up with the changing themes of finance. The repositioning of the goalposts, figuratively speaking, makes it very difficult to use the same strategy year over year and decade over decade. Therefore, you will always need to keep an eye out for the behavior of institutional traders on Wall Street who usually have first premonitions of what kind of products and securities will become popular next.

Some of the ways that industry members keep changing targets for retail investors is by showing compliance-approved hypotheticals of market or securities performance over some past time frame. The seductive marketing of the race to the bottom where fees are concerned is another way that platforms and advisors create a moving target for clients. Like the old adage says, "You get what you pay for." So in seeking out the cheapest products or platforms, be sure you are not reducing the quality of service or information you are receiving. And a final way that industry members either try to reinvent themselves, or not, for that matter, is the usage of outdated management theories. Like securities and products, the investment strategy theories that are developed by economists and the academic intelligentsia don't always stand up to the test of time. What worked twenty or thirty years ago may not work today. A new investor must relentlessly be on the search for new ideas and proactively seek them out if you do not have a financial advisor already doing so for you.

The Never-Ending Growth Chart

A prime example of changing the game over the course of time is the old trick of showing clients or prospects growth charts of the major indexes over very long periods of time, such as fifty or one hundred years. The charts like to show very concise and steady upward flow of a trend line for indexes, such as the Dow Jones Industrials or the Standard & Poor's 500. The trend line will be displayed on a graph and show a very nice, smooth line slowly growing to very significant numbers relative to the initial investment amount that was put in. Typically, these trend lines are averages that do not sufficiently show all the volatility that occurs over short time frames within the scope of the long-term view. Similarly, sometimes fund managers or product companies like to show back tested results of a certain dollar amount invested and how it hypothetically would have performed from any given point in time back through the course of their product's history.

Short-term investment evaporation

The problem with both of these portrayals is that they in no way adequately show how tumultuous the behavior is of the markets in the short-term from year to year and how wealth gets lost on market volatility during those short time intervals. And more importantly, they do not show the constant birth and death of investment product types, companies, or managed funds. The bottom line is that many products are created and then suddenly close or become defunct through the years as companies and the sectors of the economy perish due to economic crises. The fault in the provided graphs lies in their assumptions that you, as an investor, can leave positions as is over long periods of time without having to make any changes. This assumption is false and can lead to severe negative consequences for your portfolio. It could also lead to wealth destruction after a lifetime of diligent saving.

Your investing life span

Ask yourself, do you have enough time over the course of your life to wait fifty, sixty, seventy, or even eighty years to watch an investment portfolio grow to 1,000 percent gains or more? Like my own personal answer, I suspect your answer may be that you are not willing to wait that long to reap the rewards of your hard work. After all, what is the worth of extended labor if you are only able to harvest your fruits when you are too old to enjoy them? Yet that is what many of these long-term growth charts try to portray. They simply don't consider the fact that people need to live in the here and now, and need to live for the present as well as the future.

Most retail investors do not have enough wealth saved up to live off high-paying dividends and allow a separated portfolio to simply grow untouched or unmodified. For the average retail investor, most encounter some emergencies during the course of their working years where they have to withdraw funds for that emergency and, thus, interrupt the growth and compounding returns of a long-term retirement account.

The important task for you as a new investor is to seek out the kind of products you need, with your advisor, that will maximize growth for your portfolio in the shortest amount of reasonable time, such as a ten- or twenty-year time horizon. That way, you will at least be able to reap the benefits of your diligent saving. As critically important is the need to seek out patterns of short-term market cycle corrections that could destroy part of your saved wealth and subsequently force a longer time horizon to meet your goals.

You wouldn't want to push your target date for retirement out another five or ten years simply because your portfolio took a hit that was unrecoverable within a year's time. Just remember, as professionals and salesmen in the wealth management industry put performance charts in front of your eyes to make their case, always be skeptical to the root assumptions and selective data portrayal in those charts. A healthy dose of skepticism and an inquisitive nature may help you deter unsound marketing.

Dangling Carrots

With so many online trading platforms rushing to offer clients trading capability for zero commission, one may wonder what the bigger picture is. It can be tempting for any investor with the slightest bit of trading skill to jump into trading for practically no cost. However, there is one old adage that has rung true since time immemorial. That adage says, "You get what you pay for." As it held true so long ago, it holds true well through present times.

Self-trading with robo-advisors

The technical aspects of trading or investing for yourself are not hard to master with a little training and practice. Yet understanding that more than technical patterns or historical models govern the markets escapes many investors when planning for retirement and building a wealth management legacy for families or business. The short-term thrill of realizing quick gains from frequent trading often creates euphoria for the trader. But what happens when those investors lose perspective of long-term trends or refuse to look outside of one's own confirmation bias? The answer is that such investors or traders slowly become lulled into a false sense of security. It leaves them unprepared for the economic shocks that eventually rear their ugly heads every decade or so.

It is much easier to absorb portfolio losses and shocks from the short term, such as a few weeks, a few months, or even a couple of years. When a decade or a lifetime's worth of diligent, disciplined investing work suddenly becomes susceptible to market crashes, all the trading for free and do-it-yourself investing strategies become worthless. Many investors realize only then what was overlooked in the process as they perform their portfolios' postmortems in hindsight. Online brokerages and trading platforms do not sustain themselves through commissions or fees since they have other means to profit. It may be comforting as a do-it-yourself investor to have such flexibility to trade for your own portfolio. Yet all the robo-advice and marketing gimmicks from inexpensive platforms will be of no comfort when you are left to do it yourself as economic conditions turn sour during the next downturn. As an investor, how would you respond if plans head south?

Get a third-party perspective

It is always prudent to look forward to and prepare for future unknowns by benefiting from third-party perspectives. About once every decade, business models and practice trends for the financial industry morph into new paradigms by developing new products or through rebranding. Firms and investors who preempt those changes determine who will be adequately suited to weather coming storms or, at the very least, remain at the avant-garde of wealth management practice and caring for clients' futures. It is critically important to stay abreast of such changes and not be caught behind the curve when saving and planning for retirement. Perhaps the best way to prepare for such unknowns is to learn to become comfortable with uncertainty and figure out methods to plan for multiple life contingencies.

The major online trading firms, and the new ones that pop up and disappear what seems yearly now, keep enticing the general investing public with new features, tricks, and trendy yet oversimplified commercials. As for my own practice, I will remain true to the principles of steady due diligence by watching the bigger picture of market conditions and by responding smarter than chasing the hot dot on a trendy trading platform all the way down to zero. Too many financial advisors and wealth managers hear financial horror stories from clients or someone who knew someone who lost much of their savings because they refused to seek out or heed well-offered independent assessments. Instead, they relied solely on what they believed to be their own correct analysis, when in fact it was only confirmation bias as a result of small sample, short-term positive results.

Will you be adequately prepared when the time comes for the next major economic earthquake? Remember, we may not know ahead of time what will trigger the next crash, when it will start, or how long the next downturn will last. What we can be sure of is that another crash will eventually come. A good financial advisor or wealth manager can offer the thirty-thousand-foot overview of market conditions that often get overlooked by the minutiae of daily market news and the whiplash of positive to negative headlines. The dangling carrots offered by fad trading platforms will never offer you such a broad overview. Rather, they will expect you to do the legwork of research and comprehension all by yourself. While they rotate features and agreement parameters through the years, you will ultimately be stuck on a tilt-a-whirl ride that you can't get off without harm if you try.

Theoretical Rotation: MPT and Sixty-Forty

As with the 2008–2009 market crash, investors can witness a correlation among all asset classes in a downward fashion. Modern portfolio theory (MPT) and the sixty-forty portfolio balances, so commonly promoted by the major financial and academic institutions over the past several decades, have proven over the past ten years that they remain outdated models to adequately prepare investors for major shocks to their portfolios and nascent retirement security. Those who don't learn from history are bound to repeat it. MPT remained the prevailing investment theory for the past fifty years because it easily diversifies assets according to class to reduce overall risk exposure. Yet when all assets go down at the same time, the diversification of MPT ends up meaningless. This leaves the investor with a long lead time to full recovery.

What other options does an investor have? Well, as a new investor, it is important for you or the financial advisor you work with to stay abreast of the most common theories that are being developed. They will often be found among the leading economists or professors in the field of finance at Ivy League or top-tier university departments. As well, the major institutional traders of Wall Street will often be attuned to the latest theories. An easy way to get access to the fundamental studies of such people is to follow their profile on LinkedIn or their website where they publish their theories and findings on a regularly scheduled basis. I could name a few new theories that have been circulating within circles of thought in the investment world as of the writing of this book.

Alternative theoretical strategies

Some alternative strategies currently coming into focus that financial advisors and fund managers may be using are trend aggregation, adaptive optimization, and underwater correlation. Even though these terms may be confusing for a beginner, it would be worth your while to at least ask your financial professional if he understands some of these concepts. And while these specific theories may not be used by him, it is very important that he has some theoretical basis underpinning a guided strategy for your portfolio. If your advisor merely points you to some papered studies that his firm provides as part of their marketing and branding efforts, then odds are you may not have an advisor who is digging deep enough into the rigors of thought necessary to keep your investment plan ahead of the curve.

While we will not address the complex technical aspects of these theories in *Traps of Treasure*, we will say that they present innovative alternatives to the worn-out theories of the past. One of the most critical actions for any investor to understand involves coming to a self-realization of whether you make emotionally charged decisions. For those who impulsively react to the daily news without giving greater thought to the bigger picture of relevant theories, damage may occur to long-term financial security due to selling or buying at the wrong times.

Understanding one's own emotional response to panics and market shocks remains critical at this time. Volatility will always creep into the market at any given moment of time. However, it is vitally important to develop a well-thought plan of action to rise above continuous streams of negative news coming from the media. The road ahead for any wealth management plan can be bumpy back to normalcy from the depths of investment losses during a market correction, recession, or economic crisis. As a new investor, be sure to do your due diligence by finding a financial professional who does not merely utilize outdated theories. Ensure and interrogate them enough to make sure they will perform their moral duty to serve your relevant needs at your unique life moments.

CHAPTER 9

Incorruptible

Summary Points for Diving into Wealth Management

Now that we have looked at many of the pitfalls and traps a new investor can encounter when delving into wealth management, we can outline a basic approach plan. Part of this book's intent is to help you create an incorruptible and inviolable method to reach your financial dreams. If you have never worked with a financial advisor, insurance agent, or wealth manager, here is a simple breakdown of steps to start a conversation based on topics discussed in this book.

This road map can narrow down your questions and enlighten your path. It can help you decide which professional suits your personality and give you a sense of who may be a good fit to serve your needs. Even if you are experienced or already work with a financial advisor, the following steps may remind you of questions to raise with your advisor. They may need review, given the relationship's passage of time. After all, relationships change and mature through time. They are not static. Reassessing relationships every once in a while helps focus on areas for improvement for everyone involved.

A Good Starting Point

Beginning down your road to financial security, consider using the following outline to guide you:

1. Firm structure and manager type: Perform your initial research on what firm structure you prefer and which financial advisor will suit your temperament and imminent financial needs. The structure may take the form of a sole independent financial advisor specializing in one account or product type. Maybe the more appropriate structure may be a large wire house that handles multiple complex products for business dealings. Once the firm structure is selected, assess which financial advisor function you prefer. Choose whether you want an advisor who handles all the miniscule trading details and account allocation. Or if you prefer, choose an advisor who is more adept at building professional relationships. A relationship-building advisor will likely outsource day-to-day portfolio management functions to third parties and back-office support.
2. Broker transitions, retention, and protocols: Investigate how many times a financial advisor transitioned to other firms. Similarly, investigate if the firm you consider holding your assets with has a pattern of moving new brokers in and out the door quickly. You will also want to clarify the freedoms the investment firm will afford your financial advisor should the advisor choose to leave the firm. Each of these considerations can mitigate potential future disruptions to your portfolio management.
3. Moral obligations and duties: Make clear during your initial discussions with a potential advisor or firm in which capacity they will serve you. Will they serve you as fiduciaries by putting your interests first before theirs? Or will they simply function as a broker, finding you suitable investing products? Then decide how much control you wish for an advisor to have over your accounts. Do you

want to allow them discretion? Or do you prefer to call more of the shots yourself where trading and account decisions are concerned?

4. Management styles: Perform background research for yourself and discuss with your advisor whether you desire an active or passive approach to managing your account allocations. Likewise, ask the advisor about his overall philosophy toward managing. Does he prefer a technical and chart-oriented approach? Or does he prefer to assess the investing public's sentiments during different times in economic cycles? Also discuss the potential array of financial products and securities that could be made available to you.

5. Reputation: Verify if there have been any significant claims filed against the financial advisor or firm with which you intend to do business. Bear in mind though that the wealth management profession is rife with fraudulent, slanderous, libelous, and unsubstantiated claims against advisors and firms. The negative press you see at any given moment may not necessarily be true. You will have to dig a little deeper into circumstances of potential concern to see if they materially matter. Also ask your financial advisor about his communication approach and frequency with you.

6. Research and resources: Inquire of your financial advisor about his preferred data and research sources to make decisions. Specifically ask him about his methodology to avoid herd mentality regarding hot ticket securities that the media promotes with pump-and-dump schemes. You will want to ensure your advisor's view toward trading is stable and not susceptible to fleeting cultural market whims.

7. Realistic wealth expectations: Speak with your advisor at the outset of your relationship to have him quantify realistic expectations for your future wealth and retirement accounts. This will be based on your current income, accumulated assets, time horizon, and many other factors. As a client, come to the relationship with a clear mind purged of lavish excess propagated by media or advertising. The

only assets and goals of consequence are the finite and achievable ones you can reasonably expect to reach over the course of your life.
8. Stable targets: Keep an eye out through the years that advisors, fund managers, and firms do not try to change the game by swapping out methods or products you have successfully used for many years. The markets will always change over the course of your life. But you want to ensure a competent understanding of current events or theories that dictate the necessary response to such change. Beware of a firm's, fund's, or advisor's motivation to simply make more commission.
9. Security and privacy: Last, be sure to inquire of both the firm's and financial advisor's security protocols. This should be addressed from both a technology standpoint and governmental agencies standpoint. For any advisor or firm you speak with, request their disclosure brochures and their ADVs.

Minimum Expectations of Privacy and Account Security

I will offer one last remark entailing expectations an investor should have regarding personal privacy and account security. Regarding account security, almost every firm provides adequate backup systems and malware safeguards to protect your information and to ensure account integrity. Breaches of security can be rare. But when they do occur, they receive outsized attention in the media relative to how often it actually happens. As some basic guidelines for your accounts' security and personal identity protections, here are a few thoughts to consider.

Most firms will provide a direct statement as part of their regulatory disclosures. The statement addresses client privacy and how they approach it. Usually, their statements may sound something like the following:

Client privacy

> At our firm, we believe that privacy is of central importance to our relationship with you, our client. Privacy protection is a responsibility we take seriously. As our client, we are committed to safeguarding your personal information. Please read this notice entirely as it contains information regarding your rights under certain US privacy laws and our privacy policy. We may amend this notice from time to time and will provide you with a revised notice as appropriate.

Additionally, there may also be a general disclosure statement discussing more technical aspects of personal or account privacy. The attestations to confidentiality and security may sound something like the following:

> Our firm uses procedural, physical, and electronic firewall systems to store and secure information about you in compliance with federal regulations. Our systems protect your information from unauthorized access, alteration, or destruction. Access is permitted to only those individuals within our organization who need the information to perform their job responsibilities. Our firm's policy applies to anyone who is a current or former brokerage client or who registers with one of our services or promotional offers. However, the information you provide to us is equally important. This Privacy Notice is intended to provide you with a full understanding of the information we collect about you and our guidelines for sharing and safeguarding that information with others.

> We consider the information we have about you to be confidential, including the fact that you are our client. Your information will be handled in the manner described in this notice. We restrict access to information about you to those employees and authorized agents who need to know that information. We maintain physical, electronic, and procedural safeguards that comply with federal standards to maintain the confidentiality of your information.

Some privacy and security aspects will be addressed through statements of information collection, third-party disclosure, a firm's business continuity plan in case disaster strikes, and an explanation of the differences between investment brokerage firms versus banks. As a new investor, you should expect to receive these disclosures at the earliest onset of any contact, relationship, or solicitation by a financial advisor. Here are a few disclosure samples a client may see when developing a relationship with a firm or financial advisor:

Information we collect

> At our firm, we collect the following types of information about you:
>
> - Information contained in new account forms, applications, or agreements you enter into to receive our products or services, including your name, address, social security number, income, and investment objectives
> - Information about your transactions with us
> - Information from other affiliates of our firm, in accordance with that affiliate's privacy policy

- Information from other parties or sources, such as public databases

Third parties to whom we disclose information

We do not disclose your personal information to third parties, unless one of the following exceptions applies:

- We disclose personal information to investment providers that assist us in processing your transactions or servicing your account(s). An example would be a mutual fund company where you are invested that also prints and mails your account statements.
- We disclose personal information in limited circumstances when we believe in good faith that disclosure is required under law. For example, we would provide information in cooperation with security regulators or law enforcement authorities, to resolve consumer disputes, or to perform credit evaluations and authenticate checks.
- We disclose personal information to other parties as authorized by you. You may direct us, for example, to send your account statements and confirmations to third parties.

In today's rapidly changing financial markets, you want to entrust your investments to a strong partner. Our firm provides the protection you need. We view the safety and security of the assets in your accounts as a priority equal in importance to the work we do helping you build, enjoy, and share your wealth.

TRAPS OF TREASURE

Our firm's Business Continuity Plan

Our firm maintains a Business Continuity Plan in place that provides detailed steps to mitigate and recover from the loss of office space, communications, services, or key people. The Business Continuity Plan covers natural disasters, such as snowstorms, tornados, fire, and flooding. The plan covers man-made disasters, such as loss of electrical power, loss of water pressure, fire, bomb threat, nuclear emergency, chemical event, biological event, communications line outage, internet outage, railway accident, and aircraft accident. Electronic files are backed up daily and archived on- and off-site. Alternate work locations are identified to support ongoing operations in the event the main office is unavailable. It is our intention to contact all clients within five days of a disaster that dictates moving our office to an alternate location.

Differences between investment brokerage firms and banks

It is important to understand a fundamental difference between how assets are treated in a bank account versus that of a brokerage account.

Bank account. Banks are only required to have a fraction of all deposited money on hand to ensure they can meet minimum cash flow needs. Should a bank fail, and not have sufficient funds to fully reimburse its depositors, Federal Deposit Insurance Corporation (FDIC) protects depositors of member banks, up to certain limits.

Brokerage account. In the brokerage industry, on the other hand, your assets are held in custody by your brokerage firm. Unless you are using margin, we use affiliates to custody your assets, holding them on your behalf but not lending them to others. So your assets should always be available to you.

Sufficient measures to protect your assets

The assets held in an account at our firm have multiple layers of protection which include the following:

- Fiscal stewardship of our firm
- Compliance with Securities and Exchange Commission (SEC) requirements
- Coverage of Securities Investor Protection Corporation (SIPC) insurance
- Segregation of your assets from firm assets, thus protecting them from potential losses of the firm
- Full compliance with SEC rules requiring all broker-dealer firms to maintain sufficient net capital to ensure that you will get your cash and securities back, in the unlikely event that our firm should fail

At the very least, a new investor should verify that all the aforementioned protection measures are in place at a firm you choose to custody your financial assets. The measures can often be verified by looking into a firm or financial advisor's Form ADV Parts I and II. Once in a while, a rogue advisor or firm will purport to have these protections in place when in actuality they do not. It is rare, but situations of a firm's total insolvency and client asset loss can occur. When such instances occur, the former firm and its held accounts often will go into a receivership. Evidence of such instances can be found on firms' regulatory disclosure filings or legal review articles pertinent to the wealth management profession. For the most part, as a new investor, client privacy and account security should not be too much of a worry in the forefront of your mind. Everywhere I have custodied my accounts or worked for over the past twenty-five years adequately provided these protection measures.

CONCLUSION

Looking back on all the topics covered in *Traps of Treasure*, it is easy to see why there is so much confusion surrounding investing and working with financial advisors. With so many opportunities for an investor to be taken advantage of, it is hard to navigate the labyrinth of the financial world. It is my hope that you may take away enough information to help you make well-informed decisions, choose who to work with, ask targeted questions, and avoid situations that may be red flags concerning the well-being of your financial management.

As occasionally referenced in the book, several moral and biblical allegories parallel contemporary investing situations. Such allegories can help guide us through the endless traps of deception, self-interest, and fraud that make their way into the realm of wealth management. Maybe you can relate to Saul as he was blinded by a false understanding of how things really are. Or maybe you feel like Matthew in the Gospel, being called by Jesus to serve a greater purpose. There are many ways to discover your own truthful path down the road of investment management.

There are more than enough moral and benevolent financial advisors sincerely focused on getting you to a place of mental peace regarding finances. They are more than adequately equipped with resources, data, and a healthy dose of skepticism toward the games played by unethical elements of the financial world. The more ethical members of the profession will help protect and guide you toward the future. In your quest to build a financial legacy, provide for your family, and make the most of life through solid fiscal prudence, the traps and pitfalls may be many.

Yet the immaterial and abstract concepts of wealth management can turn into material and tangible products of your hard work and lifetime labors. The concepts may seem complex, mundane, or daunting at times to a new investor. But don't lose faith. In the end, with a little insight, guidance, and education, you may one day discover that the traps of treasure can instead eventually turn into trappings of treasure. They will be enshrined in a life of enjoyment, security, and devotion to those most precious and irreplaceable of commodities—namely, family, relationships, spare time, and peace of mind.

APPENDIX A

List of General Retail Investment Accounts and Products

Wealth management products

- Retirement planning
- IRAs (Roth or traditional)
- 401(k)s
- SEPs
- Simple IRAs
- Keogh (HR10)
- 403(b)
- Insurance
- Life (whole, term, and variable annuity)
- Accident
- Disability
- Long-term care
- Educational accounts
- 529 plans
- Coverdells
- UGMA/UTMA
- Employee benefit plans
- Estate planning
- Charitable giving

Account types

- Commission-based
- Fee-based
- Retirement
- Margin
- Transfer on death (TOD)

Cash products

- Check / debit card
- Rewards program
- ACH / bill pay
- Dividend reinvest
- Cash sweep

Lending products

- Commercial mortgages
- Commercial loans
- Small business association loans
- Business lines of credit
- Margin lines

Investment products

- Equities/stocks
- Large-cap equity
- Mid-cap equity
- Small-cap equity
- International equity
- Global equity
- Warrants
- Rights
- ADRs
- Restricted securities

TRAPS OF TREASURE

- Fixed income
- Bonds
- Taxable fixed income
- Tax-exempt fixed income
- High yield
- Preferred stock
- Collateralized mortgage obligations (CMOs)
- Eurodollars
- Convertible securities
- Convertible bonds
- Convertible preferred
- Mandatory convertible preferred
- Balanced funds
- Large-cap balanced
- All-cap balanced
- Global balanced
- Annuities
- Variable
- Fixed rate
- Immediate
- Unit investment trusts (UITs)
- Equity UITs
- Fixed income UITs
- Mutual funds
- Exchange traded funds (ETFs)
- Closed-end funds
- Muni-preferred
- Money markets
- Structured notes
- Money managers

APPENDIX B

Critical Questions to Ask a Financial Advisor or Investment Firm

As you venture out on your investing path, it is important to ask the right questions of a financial advisor or investment firm. As a standard of practice, a financial advisor will perform their due diligence by asking a litany of questions of new clients, such as investment time horizon, risk tolerance, sources of income, etc. However, as an investor, it is equally important that you interrogate both the financial advisor and the firm's upper management with critical questions of your own. The financial advisor or support staff may not be able to adequately answer many of your questions or the ones below. Therefore, it is important to ask these questions of a firm's principal, branch manager, regional manager, or compliance officer.

1. Q: What are the attrition and retention rates for new trainee brokers who start their career with your firm?
    Commentary: A firm with high attrition and low retention rates could indicate that advisor treatment and loyalty are problematic or abusive at that firm.
2. Q: If the financial advisor I work with leaves your firm for a competitor firm, do you permit the advisor to solicit taking me as his client to his new firm without any consequence, retribution to, or regulatory claims against the advisor?

Commentary: Ask this question explicitly of the firm's legal department and upper management. The financial advisor may be prohibited from answering this question due to compliance restrictions. If a firm comes back with an answer that this is proprietary information or that they can't answer, you should immediately eliminate this firm from consideration. A nonanswer is indicative of a firm garnishing client assets to manage at the financial advisor's expense.

3. Q: Is your firm party to the broker protocol put forth by the regulatory bodies? Or has your firm moved in and out of the broker protocol through the years?

    Commentary: Even if the firm is party, press the question to ensure the firm won't be retaliatory toward your advisor should he transition to another firm. The firm's actions could hurt your relationship with your advisor and, subsequently, result in long-term interference detrimental to your financial strategy. In other words, a firm that moves in and out of the protocol indicates a firm serving its self-interest first.

4. Q: If your firm is party to the broker protocol, how would that affect any changes my financial advisor or I make relating to your firm over time?

5. Q: Does your firm permit, then later withdrawn permission after time has passed, investment in any specific products?

6. Q: Will I be allowed to invest in the same product and types of products years from now that I potentially could invest in today through your firm?

    Commentary: If the firm cannot affirmatively answer questions 5 and 6, you will need to be vigilant to potential product-swapping shell games as time goes by, which may or may not hinder long-term portfolio performance. A firm or advisor may not have control over future availability of products provided by various investment product companies when product companies dissolve or redeem them. But some firms tend to suddenly remove products from their investment catalogue even when the investment product company still offers it for purchase and trading. Recognize the difference between the two scenarios.

7. Q: What are your firm's monthly, quarterly, and annual production quotas or targets for individual financial advisors?

    Commentary: This will often be internal information that firms will not want to disclose. If they can't answer you with either a direct answer or one that allows you to piece together the math for yourself, it could indicate the firm churns advisors frequently as production levels fluctuate through the years. Also ask them to differentiate between targets and quotas for individual advisors compared to a structured team of advisors. Some financial advisors work in partnership teams while others operate solely by themselves.

8. Q: What is the turnaround time to resolve complicated issues should my financial advisor need to speak with back-office or support team members in your various departments?

    Commentary: Turnaround time should be no more than a few days to one week for even the most complicated of issues when time is of the essence. Usual turnaround time is twenty-four to forty-eight hours for most questions, if not same day.

9. Q: As my financial advisor, will you make all the individual investment selections for my accounts? Or will that function be delegated to outside third-party managers or other managers in your firm?

    Commentary: If your financial advisor explains that he selects others to construct portfolio allocations, you may want to ensure that his fees or commissions are lower than those advisors who do make individualized recommendation decision themselves. Otherwise, you could be paying nearly double in fees.

10. Q: Does your firm limit which funds or investment types can be used in my accounts? If so, please provide me with

a categorical list of those specific funds or product companies available versus not available?

    Commentary: Some larger investment firms restrict their accounts' product access to only certain fund product companies due to long-standing, established relationships with those companies. If this is the case, you could be missing out on potentially better-performing products elsewhere. Ensure you are not limited in product offering availability. Investment firms often claim in their marketing propaganda that they offer an "open platform" with access to all product types. However, they may then later withhold recommendations or advice on those products, after they custody your assets, to reduce their liability or save the firm time.

11. Q: As a financial advisor, are you a fiduciary or not?

    Commentary: This is a critical question to ensure the financial advisor will care for your account with the appropriate level of responsibility and standard of care relative to nonfiduciary advisors.

12. Q: As a brokerage firm, do you offer discretionary accounts or are all your accounts nondiscretionary?

    Commentary: It is important to first decide as a client if you want to make the investment decisions for your account or if you want the advisor to handle that aspect. The choice holds ramifications for liability later on in the client-advisor relationship as well as broader regulatory implications.

13. Q: Do any of your firm's financial advisors' practices focus on specialized investment products or account types (i.e., self-directed IRAs, options accounts, speculative leverage accounts, 1035 exchanges, and initial public offerings)?

14. Q: As a financial advisor, do you propose a strategic or passive management investment approach or a tactical or active management approach?

15. Q: As a firm, what social media platforms or methods of communications do you permit your financial advisors to use when communicating with clients?

    Commentary: Regarding technology upgrades and communication, clearly define with your financial advisor in the beginning what your preferred communication methods are and how often it should be expected or initiated by both parties. Doing so saves a lot of stress for both parties in the long run.

16. Q: Does your firm have an internal research department of credentialed analysts or do you rely on independent third-party analysts for the source of your research to inform account management decisions?

    Commentary: Not all investment firm research departments are created equal. If the firm cannot answer that they have an extensive back-office support team of research analysts, then ensure your financial advisor or his firm provides access to reputable third-party research.

17. Q: As a financial advisor, which research material companies do you rely on to make your investment recommendations?

    Commentary: At a bare minimum, be sure your advisor utilizes at least two or three research companies for comparative studies when making portfolio recommendations.

18. Q: Does your firm offer proprietary products? If so, what kinds of investments are they?

    Commentary: If they offer proprietary products, also ask if there are minimum asset requirements to invest in them.

19. Q: Is your firm fee-based, commission-based, or a combination of the two (hybrid) when it comes to how my accounts are charged?

20. Q: As a financial advisor, how long have you been with this investment firm? How many firms have you affiliated with over the course of your entire career?

    Commentary: An advisor's tenure length with individual firms and the number of times he has switched firm affiliations can be a good predictor of the stability he offers. More frequent moves made by an advisor may indicate that you may have to redo paperwork from firm to firm. Frequent moves also make it harder to track your cost basis and cumulative performance over the years if you do not keep diligent records for yourself by retaining your monthly or quarterly statements from each firm.

21. Q: As an advisor, how often can I expect to hear from you where you initiate contact? Monthly, quarterly, twice a year, or annually?

    Commentary: Generally speaking, advisors should call every client at least once a year and update client information once every two years. Better financial advisors proactively reach out to each of their clients at least once every quarter.

22. Q: How many mergers or acquisitions of other brokers or wealth management firms or RIAs has your company been involved with over the past twenty to thirty years?

    Commentary: If the firm has acquired smaller firms, that could be an indicator of stable growth. If the firm was bought out by or merged with a bigger firm, it could portend possible structural changes. It could affect how your financial advisor serves you. The larger firm may place new terms or restrictions you didn't experience when you first began your client-advisor relationship.

23. Q: Ask your financial advisor if you can see his ADV Parts I and II as well as his FINRA BrokerCheck or SEC Investment Advisor Public Disclosure (IAPD) records?

    Commentary: These are public disclosure documents that display a financial advisor or firm's history. The documents include outside business activity, states of registration, licensure credentials, claims (true or false), and a list of firms the financial advisor has affiliated with through the years.

24. Q: Have you or your firm had claims made against you that you had to arbitrate or settle? If so, how many were

false claims that you successfully proved to be fraudulent? How many did you have to settle or pay based upon a finding against you or your firm?

Commentary: A majority of financial advisors will have had at least one or two fraudulent claims brought against them or their firm over the course of their careers. Many of the claims eventually prove to be false and get expunged from a financial advisor's record after a couple years. As an investor, you will want to look for any large (not minor) monetary settlement awards that remain on their disclosure record beyond five years from the date of the claim. As a general rule of thumb, smaller claims and fines under $10,000 that show up on a financial advisor's record usually should not be cause for significant alarm as long as the advisor can offer a clear explanation for it. Derogatory administrative comments should likewise not be of major concern as long as the advisor can offer a reasonable explanation. Regulatory agencies and unethical attorneys routinely and aggressively seek out opportunities to levy fines against financial advisors to garnish more revenue from the advisor or firm. If you need proof of this, you can reference the consistently increasing revenue and profits from year-end balance sheets from a number of various regulatory agencies.

25. Q: As a financial advisor, are you in line to succeed or inherit another advisor's book of business? Do you have any plans in the near future to merge your practice with another advisor's practice?

Commentary: This could cut both ways. If the advisor plans to buy another advisor's book of business or merge with another practice, keep an eye out so the advisor doesn't start paying less attention to you than before as he takes on more business.

26. Q: Which firm did you begin your career with and why did you leave them (if they are not still with that same firm)?

27. Q: Which licenses do you currently hold and which registration tests have you passed (i.e., the Series 6, 7, 63, 65, 66, or 24)?

    Commentary: These different Series tests will indicate what type of commissions, fees, or hourly planning the advisor is permitted to charge you.

28. Q: Do you hold any major professional designations such as Chartered Financial Professional, Accredited Wealth Manager, Accredited Investment Fiduciary, or Chartered Financial Analyst?

    Commentary: A good advisor with a strong sense of fiduciary responsibility toward clients will have at least one advanced designation, such as the ones listed above, which go above and beyond the Series tests mentioned in the previous question.

29. Q: If I have an accountant, insurance agent, real estate agent, trust administrator, executor, or other person serving as my power of attorney, will you proactively reach out to them on a consistent basis to coordinate my comprehensive wealth management strategy?

    Commentary: There is no reason for a financial advisor not to coordinate with professionals from other fields as long as the advisor has your written consent to do so. Any hint of your advisor avoiding such coordination should be a clear warning sign the advisor is avoiding effort or getting lazy in his efforts toward your wealth management plan.

30. Q: Can your firm's platform custody or household together my "held away" assets on the same monthly statements for ease of coordination and viewing of my total wealth spread out across various sources (i.e., to include annuities, other brokerage accounts, etc.)?

    Commentary: Many times, firms' platforms will be limited in what they can coordinate on monthly statements. However, finding the firm that allows you to put together more of your assets on one easy-to-read document will make it clearer for you as a client to see the bigger picture of your net worth.

31. Q: Does your firm or platform offer lines of credit collateralized against my assets held through your firm if I need to use such lines of credit in the future?

    Commentary: Lines of credit, such as margin, can be dangerous and detrimental to a client's portfolio if not used cautiously. If they do offer lines of credit, ensure your advisor does not take outsized leverage relative to the total value of your portfolio.

32. Q: Does your firm's platform offer segregated levels of access to different types of investment products based on total assets held at your firm? If so, what are the cutoff limits, minimum amount thresholds, or requirements to meet those successive barriers to entry?

    Commentary: Ideally, you will want to custody your assets with a firm that allows access to all its products to all its clients as opposed to creating preferential treatment situations for its clients with the highest amount of assets held at the firm.

33. Q: As a financial advisor, do you spend much time yourself as a chartist doing your own technical analysis or do you rely on others for your technical data and recommendations?

34. Q: Do any of your firm's principals or upper management participate on the boards or committees of the major regulatory agencies, such as FINRA, the SEC, or municipal boards?

    Commentary: This question should be asked of a firm's upper-level management. Your financial advisor may not know the exact answer to this question.

35. Q: As a financial advisor, do you retain an attorney or does your firm provide you with one to protect you from potential false claims and settlements that could be brought against your practice?

    Commentary: It is important to verify that the financial advisor you work with retains protections against false or egregious claims so those claims do not tangentially or materially impact your advisor's ability to serve you well. Even if the investment firm offers legal services to their financial advisors, a conflict of interest may still exist. Many times, investment firms will throw their advisors under the bus to protect the firm's larger interest by later refusing attorney services and protections that were initially offered to the advisor when the advisor joined the investment firm. This is a matter of frequent and costly conflict between individual advisors and investment firms when unethical clients make false claims to try to leach or extort settlement funds from an investment firm. The investment firm's attorney will often prioritize the investment firm's interest first over the financial advisor's. The attorney's salary usually comes from the firm, not the advisor. Even if you are not an interested party to a claim, your advisor may be adversely affected by such a situation. This could impact his ability to serve your financial strategy in the long run.

36. Q: Do you use any specific internal or third-party data publications or economic reports to make your strategy recommendations for my portfolio? If you do, can I also have access to the information on an ongoing basis so I can follow your thought process throughout the year?

    Commentary: As a client, you will want to ensure your advisor uses at least one or two reliable sources of information since it could affect the performance of your investment plan.

37. Q: Do you use third party fund managers as part of your portfolio allocation process? If you do, can I see their performance track records thoroughly broken down over multiple time horizons, such as quarterly, one-year, three-year, five-year and ten-years or longer if such records exist?

38. Q: Have you ever used speculative positions (i.e., initial public offerings, over-the-counter/pink sheet stocks, blue-skied securities or other like-kind products) to improve performance in any of your clients' accounts? If so, can

you tell me what those positions were, when they were acquired, when they were sold and whether it resulted in profits or losses?

Commentary: If the advisor gives you some of this information, which they may not be allowed to per their compliance restrictions, you will want to thoroughly trace back the information to see how the position played out over different time frames. Short-term stellar results may be fine at one moment, but they can quickly turn disastrous during other time frames or events in market cycles.

39. Q: As a financial advisor, do you provide access to trusts or expertise regarding my particular circumstances?

    Commentary: Sometimes a financial advisor will be able to address specific needs that don't always show up in the general investing population. Such specific concerns could include divorce planning, generation skipping transfers, and overseas accounts, to name a few examples.

40. Q: As a financial advisor, are you familiar with the particular issues concerning different professions (i.e., physicians, lawyers, engineers, accountants, teachers, and entertainers)?

    Commentary: Certain highly skilled professions or professions that accumulate large amounts of assets in short amounts of time may need specialized attention from an advisor. Oftentimes, financial advisors will focus their book of business around a niche of client types in one profession or another. Try to determine if your financial advisor is a specialist serving clients from certain professions or if he is more of a generalist with a wide variety of client types. If your profession is highly specialized, it may be beneficial to find an advisor who understands the schedule, rhythms, time constraints, or needs of your particular profession.

41. Q: As a financial advisor, can you work around my work schedule, even outside of typical market trading hours, to accommodate me and speak with me even if I may not be reachable during usual business and market trading hours?

Commentary: This question may be very applicable to professionals such as doctors or those with long or unusual business hours where they can't be reached by telephone during standard market hours. You will need to establish a clear means of immediate communication with your financial advisor. It may become critical during times of great market volatility or economic crises. Not always, but sometimes time can be critical in these instances.

ABOUT THE AUTHOR

Louis Scherschel practiced as a private wealth manager for over thirteen years until his retirement to pursue other passions. In 2009, he entered the private wealth management field with the Royal Bank of Canada where he worked for several years in its US Wealth Management division. He subsequently set out on his own in independent practice until retirement. From the time he entered the wealth management industry in the depths of the 2009 financial crisis, Louis honed an approach toward wealth management to offer investors a moral compass currently lacking in the industry. He delineated a well-lit path navigating the industry's unethical behaviors perpetually practiced upon unsuspecting investors.

Enlightening the general public about less commonly known aspects of investment firm operations remains a passion for Louis. He takes this educational process seriously as a moral obligation to the general public. One of his aims is bringing to light how many financial institutions fail to disclose strategies, methods, or products, which could hinder or help building a wealth legacy. As well, his investigations look behind the opaque curtain of what occurs within many financial service entities. Through his insights accumulated during his tenure in the financial field, Louis previously guided individuals through the investing world's obscured maze.

Louis's educational background includes degrees in civil engineering and architecture, in addition to preparations for financial advisory licensure. Due to the path he took to enter wealth management, Louis brought a unique vantage point not offered by the cookie-cutter professionals die-cast from the outmoded, insular, and entitled cliques of Wall Street. Too often, those isolated networks appear more interested in enriching themselves at the expense of the retail investing public. His outsider's view offers invaluable perspective to cut through overplayed taglines and deceptive lures frequently pitched by the majority of the investment industry. Louis Scherschel currently lives in metropolitan Chicago where he continues his professional passions in the design field.

www.ingramcontent.com/pod-product-compliance
Lightning Source LLC
Chambersburg PA
CBHW020916180526
45163CB00007B/2761